595
S0-AEM-420

THE PARTHENON FRIEZE

text: Martin Robertson
photographs: Alison Frantz

PHAIDON

in association with
British Museum Publications Limited

to Bernard Ashmole

Acknowledgements

We owe thanks for permission to illustrate material in their charge, and for much help and kindness, to Denys Haynes, until lately Keeper of the Department of Greek and Roman Antiquities at the British Museum, John Miliades of the Acropolis Museum, and the late Jean Charbonneaux and Pierre Devambez of the Louvre; and to Homer Thompson for constant help and encouragement. The American Philosophical Society provided generous financial aid towards the photography, and for this too we are most grateful. The dedication to Bernard Ashmole acknowledges a larger debt as well as warm affection.

MARTIN ROBERTSON

ALISON FRANTZ

Phaidon Press Limited, Littlegate House, St Ebbe's Street, Oxford
First published 1975

©1975 by Phaidon Press Limited

Reprinted 1976

All rights reserved

ISBN 0 7148 1659 0

No part of this publication may be reproduced, stored in a retrieval system or transmitted in any form or by any means, electronic, mechanical, photocopying, recording or otherwise, without the prior permission of the Copyright owner

Printed in Great Britain by T. and A. Constable Ltd., Edinburgh

Foreword

Like the Sistine ceiling or Shakespeare's sonnets, the Parthenon frieze is a familiar and manifestly wonderful work which yet remains in many aspects baffling. A great deal has been written about it, and it is safe to say that a great deal more will be written, but there is no certainty about exactly what is represented and it is hardly possible that we shall ever know. The *raison d'être* of this book is the splendid series of photographs by Alison Frantz, to which it is my privilege to supply a commentary. The frieze is a consistent unity, clearly distinct in subject and presentation from the other sculptures of the building. It is given here in its full surviving length, outline drawings indicating portions which are lost but whose composition was recorded before their disappearance, and those places noted where slabs have perished without trace; and detail photographs from different parts display the quality and variety of the work. The full length was similarly presented, along with the other sculptures, in two French publications of 1910 and 1912, listed in the bibliography; but the pictures are small and the books large; there is much less range of detail; and the publications are not now available easily, if at all. Many other books show many parts of the frieze, often finely, but this is the only modern monograph which gives it complete.

In the captions I have discussed points of detail, and in the introductory essay have indicated the variety of interpretations offered for the subject represented and dwelt rather longer on the one I prefer. I have chiefly concentrated, however, on the broader background in four aspects: first, the historical and social development against which the marble adornments of the Acropolis were brought into being; second, the peculiar character of that building and of its relation to the huge image for which and with which it was constructed; third, the frieze in the context of the whole sculptural decoration of the Parthenon; and finally the later history and influence of the frieze.

MARTIN ROBERTSON

Lincoln College, Oxford
1974

Historical background

'The Acropolis' means to us the Acropolis of Athens; but *akropolis* is a common Greek noun, meaning 'upper city' or 'citadel'. Almost every city of Greece had an area to which that name could be applied: a defensible centre, which also had, as a rule, religious associations. The acropolis formed one of the centres of city life, the other being the *agora*, a word often translated 'market-place', which indeed it was, but it was more – a focus of social and political activity; and it, too, commonly included holy spots. The reason that the Athenian acropolis is for us the 'Acropolis' *par excellence* lies in its adornment: the four marble buildings set there in the second half of the fifth century B.C., of which the first and greatest is the temple of Athena known as the Parthenon. One part of the Parthenon's rich sculptural decoration is the subject of this book; but before we come to that a word is needed on the social and historical development which led to the transformation of the citadel of Athens into the Acropolis we know.

Athens was a city already in the Bronze Age, and the Acropolis its citadel: an embattled castle like those of Mycenae and Tiryns. When Greece begins to emerge into history in the eighth and seventh centuries B.C., Athens is found in the pattern of other Greek city-states: a city, controlling a considerable area of countryside (Attica), and governed by an oligarchy, a caste of landed families in whose hands were concentrated alike wealth and all state and religious offices. Economic and social crises led in Athens, as in many other Greek cities, to the setting up of a 'tyranny' – one man (in Athens, Pisistratus) using popular discontent with the oligarchic establishment to seize power for himself. In Athens, however, this stage was delayed by a modification of the constitution in the interest of a wider range of people carried through at the beginning of the sixth century by Solon, himself like Pisistratus a member of the oligarchy. Solon was later looked back to as the father of Athenian democracy; but the full democratic constitution which was to remain in force, with modifications and brief interruptions, as long as the city retained her independence was only established, by another oligarch, Clisthenes, at the end of the century, after the expulsion of Pisistratus' sons. Meanwhile the tyrants had made Athens a literary and artistic centre, and raised on the Acropolis temples which, in their grandeur and elaboration (revealed to us in ruined fragments), anticipated the achievements of the classical age.

During this time the Greek cities of the eastern Aegean, the west coast of Asia Minor and the islands off it, had become absorbed in the western spread of the Persian empire. In 499 B.C. many of them rose in revolt, with the help from beyond the Aegean of Eretria in Euboea and of Athens. The revolt was suppressed, and in 490 Darius sent a punitive expedition which razed Eretria and landed in Attica. The Persians were put to flight at Marathon, and newly democratic Athens thus became the first Greek state to inflict a decisive defeat on the might of Persia. In the following years the city, under the leadership of Themistocles and with wealth from the silver mines at Laurium and the Attic olive-groves, built up a powerful fleet; and when, in 480, Xerxes led a huge force to incorporate mainland Greece in the empire, Athens was accepted as fellow-leader of the resistance with Sparta, the most prestigious of Greek cities. After the destruction of his fleet at Salamis in 480, and a crushing defeat by land at Plataea in 479, the invader withdrew; but Athens had been laid waste, the buildings and monuments in the upper and lower city burned and razed. The victorious Greeks (who, at about the time of Plataea, had destroyed a second Persian fleet at Mycale east of the Aegean) formed a confederacy, based on the holy island of Delos, devoted to freeing the eastern Greeks from Persia, but Sparta soon lost interest, and leadership of the mainly maritime league devolved on Athens. During the seventies and sixties the object of the league was largely achieved, but over the same period its character began to undergo a change. Cities other than Athens moved more and more from contributing ships and men to contributing money; cities which did not wish to join or wished to leave were constrained to be members; and in 454 the treasury was transferred from Delos to Athens. The Delian League was well on its way to becoming an Athenian empire. The final step came a few years later, when Pericles carried, against bitter criticism often echoed since, a proposal to apply the funds of the league to rebuilding the temples on the Acropolis which had lain in ruin for a generation. It appears, though the evidence is obscure and the facts disputed, that the Greek armies before Plataea had taken an oath not to rebuild the temples and shrines destroyed by the barbarian but to let them stand as a warning; and that in 449 a formal treaty (the Peace of Callias) was concluded with the Persian King Artaxerxes, in which the freedom of the eastern Greek cities, won by the Athenians and their allies, was recognized; and that this assurance of peace was held to absolve the Greeks from their oath. In any case the Periclean building-programme, in both upper and lower city, was launched at just this time.

Fifth-century Athens

Fifth-century Athens was a democracy. The word *demokratia* (people's rule) was that used by the Greeks themselves, and the Athenian constitution was the ancestor of 'democracy' in the various forms in which we understand that equivocal concept; but it did not much resemble any modern manifestation. In all Greek states one main foundation of social and economic life was slavery; women were without political rights; and resident aliens (metics), though in Athens they had special privileges and duties going back to Solon's legislation, were not citizens. The little that is known of the status of the men who actually built and adorned the Parthenon will be touched on later. What made Athens a democracy was the fact that the governing body was the Assembly formed of all adult male citizens; and that holders of public office were appointed from that body by a complicated system of ballot and lot. All were in theory eligible, but until well into the second half of the fifth century the great figures who guided the city's policy were in practice drawn almost exclusively from the old families. Such were Cimon, who led the war against Persia in the east, and Pericles, whose influence was almost continuously predominant through the forties and thirties. He set Athens on the collision course with Sparta which culminated in the long, disastrous Peloponnesian War, at the beginning of which he himself died; and he organized the great building scheme and the devotion to it of the allies' tribute; but everything was done by decree of the Assembly.

The lower city had been built under Themistocles and Cimon, and shrines of Theseus and the Dioscuri erected there and adorned with wall-paintings. Work had been done on the Acropolis, too: the great south wall and the terracing behind it are Cimonian, and he probably also put up a monumental gate-house; but it is generally held, I believe rightly, that the temples had been left as the Persians ruined them. The new programme began just after the mid century (I suppose after the Peace of Callias in 449) with the decreeing of two temples, one in the lower, one in the upper city. That in the lower was the Temple of Hephaestus (in whose worship Athena was associated as patroness of craftsmen): the building long mistakenly known as the Theseum, which still stands, the best-preserved temple in Greece, on a mound above the west side of the Agora. That on the Acropolis was the Parthenon.

Predecessors of the Parthenon

The clearing, terracing and new building which took place on the Acropolis in the fifth century have made it impossible to recover much of its archaic layout. Substantial fragments exist of sixth-century architectural sculpture; some from small buildings which can hardly have been temples, but more than one temple is evidenced by the larger remains. One cannot tell, however, whether these remains adorned buildings succeeding one another on one site, or buildings erected at different times to stand alongside one another. It is certain that one temple lay near the centre of the rock: its foundations are to be seen today, north of the Parthenon and just south of the Erechtheum, which was built in the last quarter of the fifth century. It is virtually certain too that this was the principal temple and housed the most holy object in Athenian religion: an olive-wood image of Athena, believed to have fallen from heaven in the reign of the legendary king Erechtheus. It can further be said that this temple was standing at the time of the Persian occupation (when the image was taken to the island of Salamis, one of the places to which Athenian families were evacuated), and the building burned; that on the return the image was housed for many years in some temporary shelter, probably erected on the old site; and that when a temple was at last built to be its home and replace the ancient one, it was not the Parthenon but the Erechtheum.

It is also known that at the time of the sack a temple was under construction on the site now occupied by the Parthenon. The platform was built, partly founded on the rock, but artificially terraced out to the south, and work had begun on the lower courses. Some drums from the columns, still unfluted, were built into the north wall of the Acropolis after the return and can still be seen. What is wholly uncertain, and much debated, is whether this unfinished pre-Persian temple stood on an ancient holy spot where a temple had stood before, or was the first on the site. The Parthenon we know incorporates the platform of its immediate predecessor, and the plan of that (different from and more conventional than that of the extant building) is in great part recoverable; but the earlier history of the site is concealed beneath these. The question whether a temple stood there, or a building of a different kind, or more than one building, or nothing, must remain open.

There is further doubt about the history of the temple after the Persian sack. The opinion I have followed in this outline is the commonly, and I believe rightly, accepted one: that the ruins lay untouched until the Periclean building was decreed in 449 B.C. It has recently been argued, however (the Plataean Oath and its recantation after the Peace of Callias dismissed as figments), that in the sixties Cimon began and carried far towards completion a temple on the platform and plan of the pre-Persian building; and that much of this work survives in the Parthenon we have. Ancient authorities tell us that two architects worked on the Parthenon, Callicrates and Ictinus; and on this theory Callicrates was the author of Cimon's temple, Ictinus of Pericles'; and the change of architect and plan was one manifestation of a political and personal feud between the two leaders. Rhys Carpenter, the doyen of classical art historians, who has put this view forward, supports it with a dazzling display of arguments, archaeological, art-historical and political, but it remains to me finally unconvincing.

These are questions of much interest in themselves; but happily the answers, or lack of answers, to them do not affect the facts about the Periclean Parthenon which are most important for our study: first, that this building was never intended to take the place of the ancient and most holy temple of Athena in her city, the home of the olive-wood image; and then that it has many peculiar features which set it off from any other Greek temple, among them the frieze.

Parthenon and Parthenos

Many of the peculiarities of the Periclean Parthenon can be traced to the fact that its building was contemporaneous with and intimately linked to the construction by Phidias of the huge image of Athena, veneered in gold and ivory, which was known as the Parthenos. The Doric temple, from the time it assumed its canonical form a century and a half or two centuries before, was always conceived primarily as the house of the deity, personified in a statue. Sacrifice and ritual took place largely outside, round the altar, which commonly stood opposite the main entrance of the temple, at the east end. Within the surrounding colonnade a columned porch led into a long, narrow room, normally occupying most of the length of the building, and often further narrowed by a row of inner columns down each side, at the end of which stood or sat the image of the deity, facing the east door and the approaching worshipper. The statue in an archaic temple seems normally to have been life-size or a little over. Colossal figures were made then, like the marble Apollo of the Naxians at Delos, or the bronze-clad Apollo of Amyclae near Sparta, but these stood in the open air. It is only in the mid fifth century that we begin to hear of colossal cult-statues within temples: an Athena at Plataea, of gilded wood with marble face and hands; the Parthenos at Athens and the Zeus at Olympia, whose veneer was of ivory and gold; all three the work of Phidias. Gold and ivory had been used for life-size statues in the archaic period; the colossal temple-statue in precious materials appears to be an innovation of this time, particularly associated with Phidias. That he was not himself entirely responsible, however, is suggested by a nice story that he told the Athenians that marble was cheaper than ivory and would last better.

The Parthenos was some forty feet high; the Zeus much the same but even larger in scale since he was seated while the goddess was standing. The Zeus was placed in a temple of strictly conventional design. This building was finished by 456, some years before the Parthenon was begun, but it is now virtually certain that the statue was not made for it until after the lapse of a quarter of a century. The Zeus seems to have been universally felt in later antiquity to be the greater of the two statues; but at least one observer accuses Phidias of failing to observe a proper proportion in setting so huge a figure under the low ceiling of a temple's narrow room. Parthenos and Parthenon were under construction together, and many of the oddities of the building seem designed to give a freer space to the colossal statue. The Temple of Zeus at Olympia, and in Athens the Temple of Hephaestus by the Agora, built at the same time as the Parthenon, each have six columns at the ends and thirteen down the sides. The six at the ends is almost universal in classical Doric, but the number along the sides varies. The older Parthenon had six by sixteen, an unusually long and narrow form; the Periclean, most abnormally, eight by seventeen. Both had exceptionally shallow porches at either end, and an unusual internal division. Normally the east porch is balanced by a false porch at the west (so the Temple of Zeus at Olympia and that of Hephaestus at Athens). In both phases of the Parthenon the west porch led into a squarish room, but this had no access to the main temple-room with its internal colonnade, which was entered by its east porch. In the early building this eastern room, owing to the great overall length of the temple, was of normal proportion. In the Periclean form it is exceptionally wide for its length and made more so by the fact that the internal colonnade turns round the west end behind the statue-base.

This room is a hundred Attic feet long (the Attic foot was slightly longer than the modern). We hear of an archaic temple on the Acropolis known as the Hekatompedon ('the Hundred-foot'). This may be the old temple whose foundations remain; they measure about a hundred Attic feet over all; but it has been argued that the original Hekatompedon lay under the Parthenon. The name 'Parthenon' was originally applied only to the back room of the Periclean and pre-Periclean buildings. *Parthenos* means 'maiden', and since Phidias' statue was known as 'the Parthenos' or 'Athena Parthenos' one might naturally assume that this was a cult-title of Athena as worshipped here, and the name of the building derived from that. There is, however, no evidence for the use of this cult-title. The word *parthenōn* is of the same kind as *gynaikōn*, 'women's quarters', and *andrōn*, 'men's quarters' (hence 'dining-room'), and would naturally mean 'maidens' quarters'. It may be that there was an archaic building of this name, for priestesses or virgins engaged in the cult of Athena, possibly under part of the site of the temple, and that the back room in the earlier Parthenon was originally intended for that use; in the Periclean building it seems always to have served as a treasury. When the name had become extended to the building as a whole, *Parthenos* as an identifying title for this statue of Athena would have derived from that. There were many other statues of the goddess on the Acropolis, at least two of them, Promachos and Lemnia, by Phidias; and at least three other statues of her by the same artist in other places.

Adornment of statue and building

The design of the Parthenon was surely influenced by the fact that it was meant to house, and was erected at the same time as, the Parthenos; and the special relation was carried on in the adornment of the two creations. The areas of a Doric temple which might bear sculptural decoration were early established and seldom varied. All were high up on the building and on the outside; or at least, if within the surrounding colonnade, on outward-facing walls. A Doric temple – and in the aspects here considered the Parthenon follows normal conventions – stands on a stepped platform from which smooth walls and fluted columns rise directly without any intervening base-moulding. The simple capitals of the columns support a plain beam, the architrave or epistyle, and above that comes the frieze. This word is properly an architectural term defining this level in a classical building, however treated. In Doric it is normally divided into alternate triglyphs and metopes (so, the outer face of the Parthenon): the triglyph an upright rectangle, vertically grooved, one above each column, one between; the metope a squarish panel, plain or (as on the Parthenon) carved with figures. This is the lowest level on a Greek temple at which sculpture is canonically

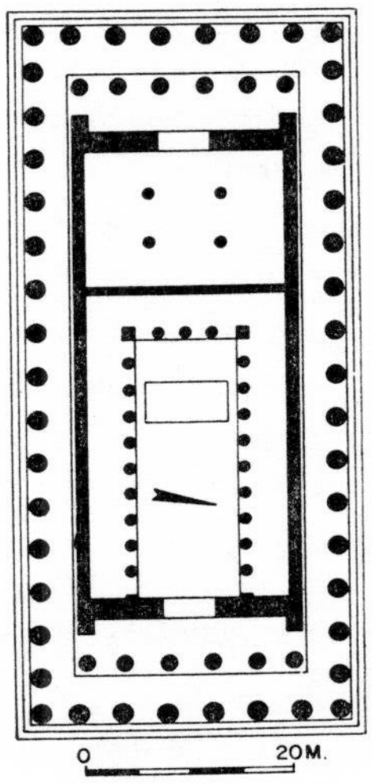

Plan of the Parthenon

The Doric Order

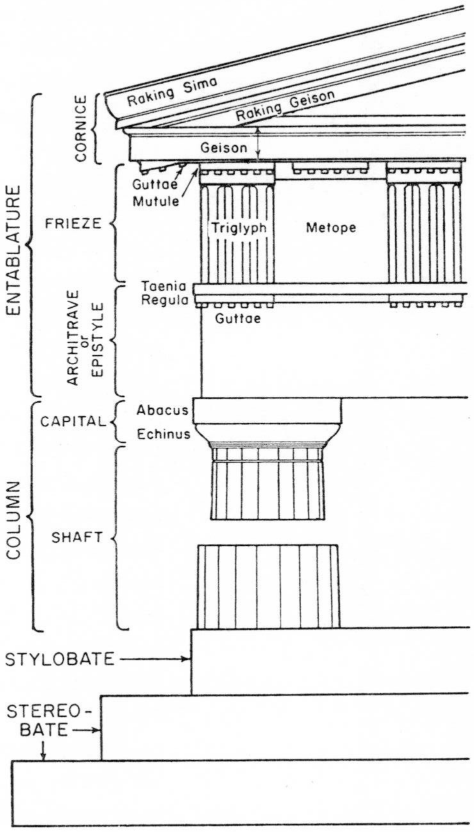

admitted. In Ionic (the closely related but more elaborate architectural order, developed east of the Aegean while Doric was perfected on the mainland and in the west) this level is often decorated with a continuous carved band. On several mid-fifth-century Doric temples in Athens and Attica, which preserve metopes and triglyphs on the exterior, such a band is used instead of these at the same level over the porches at back and front within the outer colonnade; and on the Parthenon it is carried down the long sides as well, so completely surrounding the inner building. By extension the word 'frieze' is used for any long band carved, or even painted, with figures, and this is now the most normal usage. 'The Parthenon Frieze' now means the continuous band, as against the metopes of the exterior; and I use it so here.

Above this level comes the cornice, crowned by a gutter pierced with rain-vents which are often, as on the Parthenon, carved as lion-heads. The roof slopes back from the gutter on the long sides, forming at the ends low gables, the pediments, framed by the horizontal cornice below and raking cornices (with false gutters) above. These pediments are the second great area for sculptural decoration; the third and last (apart from the lion-head rain-spouts) is higher still: *akroteria*, free-standing sculptures above the three angles of each gable.

These were all permissible areas for sculpture, but many temples were without decoration of this kind at all, and very few had it in all possible places. The early fifth-century temple of Aphaia on Aegina had figured akroteria and pediments but the metopes were left plain. On the temple of Zeus at Olympia the metopes of the outer circuit were plain but the six over each porch carved and the pediments filled with sculpture. In this case akroteria were added later. The Parthenon was not only of exceptional size and built and adorned entirely in marble (a departure in Doric though long practised in the rich cities of archaic Ionia), but of all temples we know was the most fully adorned with sculpture. The akroteria were floral; but figure-scenes were found not only in the pediments but in all ninety-two metopes of the exterior colonnade as well as all round the inner building in the continuous frieze. The marble for building and sculpture alike came from quarries still to be seen on Mount Pentelikos (the modern Pendeli) to the north-east of Athens. This is white when cut, but weathers to a warmer, sometimes golden colour.

The subject-matter of the sculptures on a Greek temple has not always much connection with the deity worshipped there. Aphaia was a local Aeginetan goddess, sometimes identified with Artemis; but the gables of her temple show heroic battles, and the deity who takes the centre in both is not Aphaia nor Artemis but Athena, patroness of heroes, and she appears in the same position on a late archaic temple of Apollo at Eretria. Apollo himself seems to have dominated the east gable of his late archaic temple at Delphi, as Zeus does on his early classical one at Olympia; but in the west gable at Olympia Zeus yields the centre to Apollo, and the metopes have the labours of Hercules, helped by Athena and Hermes. Both pediments of the Parthenon glorified

Athena: the east showed her miraculous birth from the head of Zeus, the west her successful strife with Poseidon for the land of Attica. The subjects of the metopes are not so directly illustrative of Athena's legend, but they are linked in what cannot be a chance way to the adornments of the great statue of the goddess by Phidias within.

The new concept of the colossal cult-statue presented new problems and new opportunities; and Phidias made both his Athena and his Zeus not only images of the deity but vehicles for a wealth of subsidiary narrative decoration. The Parthenos stood with her shield resting beside her on the ground. Its inside was painted with the battle of the Gods and Giants (Gigantomachy); its outside carved with a battle of Greeks and Amazons (Amazonomachy). The metopes at east and west of the building are very much defaced, but it is certain that those on the east showed the Gigantomachy, virtually certain that the combats on the west are of Greeks and Amazons. Round the rims of the statue's sandals was shown a battle of Greeks and Centaurs (Centauromachy); and this reappears in the only well-preserved metopes of the building, which come from the two ends of the south side (where the metopes in between, lost and known only in drawings, showed, rather oddly, some other now obscure subject). The ruined metopes of the north showed another favourite legend of Greek heroic glory, the sack of Troy (Iliupersis). This had no counterpart on the statue, but the scenes of the sack appear to have been framed by a metope on the left with Helios (the Sun) in his chariot, and one on the right with Selene (the Moon) on a horse. The same two figures similarly framed the scene on the front of the statue-base, the creation of Pandora, as they did also that of the birth of Aphrodite on the base of the Zeus at Olympia; and they reappear framing the birth of Athena in the east gable of the Parthenon, though there Selene too is in a chariot.

The birth of Athena though popular in archaic art, especially in Athens, had become a rare subject by this time; the strife of Athena and Poseidon is very rare at all periods; but these, like the rest of the decoration and like all temple-adornment before and almost all after, are drawn from the stock of mythology and legend. The subject of the frieze, a religious procession, is unique in such a context, as indeed is almost every aspect of this extraordinary monument.

The frieze: organization and subject

A continuous frieze on one face of a Greek temple is normally concerned with a single subject, but if all the faces of a building are so adorned the subjects of the four stretches are often independent and unconnected. Even where one subject occupies all four faces, as the battle of Greeks and Amazons, for instance, seems to have done at one level on the Mausoleum of Halicarnassus in the following century, overall unity is achieved by the varied repetition of certain basic patterns of grouping, not by the subordination of all sides to a single design embracing the whole. Such a design, developed over all four sides through figures of different kinds variously engaged but all united in one purpose, is found in the Parthenon frieze, and it has no parallel. The procession is shown on the two long sides, facing east, the varied participating groups loosely but not mechanically balanced on north and south; and round the corners on the east end appear the two heads of the procession to left and right, each facing a group of seated deities, who face them as the statue in a temple faces the worshippers. At the back of the procession are long rows of Knights on horseback, and more of these, loosely grouped, some mounted some preparing themselves or their beasts, occupy the west face. At the very centre of the east end, between the backs of the two groups of seated gods, is another small group of five standing mortals, concerned with some ritual which must be the end and object of the procession.

There were many great religious festivals celebrated in Athens, not a few of them concerned with the city's goddess as she was worshipped on the Acropolis. No doubt a procession was often included; but there was one feast of peculiar importance in which a procession played an integral part. Every summer, on the twenty-eighth of the month Hekatombaion (which ran from July into August), considered to be Athena's birthday, was held the Panathenaia; and every fourth year the Great Panathenaia, at which a procession of citizens conducted to the Acropolis a robe, woven (by those of their daughters honoured with the task) with the battle of Gods and Giants, and it was wrapped about the olive-wood image. The Panathenaia seems to have been of immemorial antiquity. Its foundation is ascribed to the legendary king Erechtheus, in whose reign the image had fallen from heaven, no doubt on this very day. The Great Panathenaia was the creation of Pisistratus, on the model of the four-yearly festivals at Olympia and Delphi, perhaps in 566 B.C. He seems at the same time and on the same models to have reorganized and regularized the contests which formed part of the festival, and to have inaugurated the giving of prizes (Attic olive-oil) in painted jars of particular form and design. At the time of the Parthenon these vessels were still being made and decorated with the inscription and designs established by Pisistratus, and in the 'black-figure' technique flourishing at that time but long gone out of fashion; indeed they were still being so made centuries later, when there was no other Greek vase-painting and Athens was no longer mistress of an empire or even an independent city, but continued to honour the goddess with festival, procession and robe.

This was certainly the greatest single religious event in the Athenian cycle, and the identification of the procession shown in defiance of tradition on the great temple on the Acropolis with the Panathenaic procession is almost irresistible. There are arguments against it, but those in its favour seem to me overwhelming. To take the counter-indications first: some elements which we know were present in the actual Panathenaic procession are omitted from the representation on the frieze – the 'Panathenaic ship', and a group of citizens marching as 'hoplites', the heavy-armed infantry which was the backbone of every Greek army. The Panathenaic ship was a ship on wheels, with a mast on which the new robe was hoisted and so displayed as the procession passed through the city. It was moored at the foot of the Acropolis, and the robe carried on by hand. Evidence about the vessel is late, and it is not quite certain that it formed part of the procession at this time. A like ship-cart of Dionysus is, however, shown on an Athenian vase of the early fifth century dedicated on the Acropolis, and it is probable that the wheeled vessel with the robe for sail was an original part of the Panathenaic procession. Its omission from the Parthenon frieze as we have it can hardly be accounted for by destruction. Short stretches are lost without record, but none in which it is possible to find a place for such a representation. Indeed it is not easy to envisage such an object rendered at all within the conventions of the frieze-carving; and that surely is the true explanation of its omission. The frieze represents a procession, but it is not a documentary record. It is, as we shall see when we consider it more closely, a highly sophisticated work of art, and as such highly selective; and this selectivity no doubt accounts also for the omission of a contingent of citizens marching in armour. The designer gave over a high proportion of the whole to his marvellously decorative evocations of horsemen and chariots, and confined his choice of those to be represented on foot to certain classes of civil participants. A different argument urged against the identification is the fact that the image for which the robe was meant was never housed in the building the frieze adorns. Parthenos and Parthenon, however, were devoted with great consistency to the glory of Athena as patroness of Athens, and the most holy embodiment of that presence was the olive-wood figure. The representation around this building of the procession to bring that image its robe fitly links the resplendent ivory and gold within to the ancient holiness. One may note also that the battle of Gods and Giants, woven into the robe, reappeared painted within the statue's shield and carved on the façade of the building.

The departure from the tradition of decorating temples only with scenes from mythology must imply that the activity represented was of exceptional sacred importance, as was the Panathenaic procession; and that it is indeed that procession which is shown here is clinched by the character of the little scene at the centre of the east end, isolated by the groups of gods. Here a woman, a priestess it must be, takes a stool from the head of a young girl, another approaching with a second. Back to back with the priestess is a man in a long-sleeved robe, not a priest, since there was no priest of Athena, but an officer of state, no doubt the *Archon Basileus* ('King Minister'), a politically powerless but most holy office, the last embodiment in the democracy of legendary kingship in its religious aspect. He it was who chose the girls to weave the robe; and the man on the frieze is taking from or handing to a child a large square of folded cloth. There can be no certainty about the exact meaning of the actions in this little scene, though we shall have to consider them further, but the piece of stuff must surely be the *peplos*, the robe.

Execution and design: position and appearance

We know a good deal about the progress of work on statue and building, in part from literary references, more from fragmentary inscriptions found on the Acropolis, in which were recorded authorizations of expenditure. Work was begun in 447 B.C. and completed fifteen years later. The Athenians distinguished years by the name of the chief magistrate, and the list can be equated with other systems giving firm dates. The statue was dedicated in 438/7, and by then the roof must have been on, so the slabs at frieze-level must have been laid somewhat earlier. The metopes of the outer colonnade were certainly carved before being put in position, but the continuous frieze, along the long sides, was with equal certainty carved *in situ*; not therefore during the earlier years of work on the building. These slabs are of a regular size, about four feet long, and the design does not respect the slab-divisions. Most of the slabs on the east are much larger, and both here and on the west there is much less overlapping of figures from one to another, so that it is possible that these were carved before being set in place. Detailed studies have distinguished many hands at work on the frieze, and these are sometimes referred to as 'masters', but this is misleading. A large body of craftsmen must have worked on the execution, and they can be distinguished by mannerisms, but the consistently high quality shows that they were very well trained. Further, the harmony of the style shows that they followed accurately detailed designs which, if not all the work of one artist, must at least have been closely checked by one man who had given the programme and sketch for the whole. From the end of the century we have an inscription recording payment for the execution of a frieze of the Erechtheum. Here named men receive money at a fixed rate (60 *drachmai* per figure), half a dozen men producing separate figures for a single scene, the harnessing of a chariot, where they must have been working to an exact given design. The cases are not identical, since the friezes of the Erechtheum (which are much smaller than those of the Parthenon) are in a peculiar technique: slabs of dark Eleusinian stone to which were attached figures carved separately in white marble. Division of labour on the Parthenon frieze is more likely to have been by lengths of slab than by figures, but the principle must have been the same. Distinction of designation among the names in the Erechtheum inscription shows that some of the executants were Athenian citizens, others not, and the same no doubt was true of the workers on the earlier building. The metopes of the Parthenon show very considerable variety of style and of quality. By the time work on the frieze started it is clear that the team had been trained to a high degree of competence and understanding.

The frieze is rather over three feet high, and originally covered a length of some 524 feet. About 420 feet survive, and over fifty more are recorded in drawings. The slabs are carved in low relief. In high relief (an art-form developed by the Greeks during the archaic period and found on the Parthenon in the metopes) the forms are given their full three-dimensional, sculptural, value, but the figures are composed in a two-dimensional composition against the background from which they are not cut free. In low relief, a much older tradition, the forms are distorted towards the flatness of a drawing. Indeed low relief is often nearer in the character of its conventions to drawing than to sculpture in the round. This is the case with much archaic Greek work. Classical low relief is generally more fully modelled, but there is nothing to equal the sophisticated variety and richness of treatment on the Parthenon frieze: a three-quartered face given almost its full sculptural value, a foreshortened foot hardly more than drawn in the marble; yet all harmoniously united. The depth of the relief is never more than two or three inches, and tends to be greatest towards the top of the slab, evidently to help the effect from below.

It is often suggested that the frieze, some forty feet up within the roofed colonnade, will have been virtually invisible. The west frieze, still in position, is now open to the sky, so that one cannot judge the original effect, but I am told that when it was planked over during restoration work it told well in the reflected light from below. This was in any case a favourite position for sculpture on a Greek temple, at the ends of the building though not along the sides: so, the metopes at Olympia and many others. It is true that these are in high relief, and indeed that high relief seems to have been evolved by the Greeks partly because all the regular positions for sculpture on their buildings were high up, far from the eye; but the unique character of the low relief on the Parthenon frieze is surely developed likewise just for this reason. It will, too, like all Greek sculpture, have been coloured. The dark stone of the Erechtheum frieze-slabs corresponds to a wash of colour on the background of marble reliefs, often blue on grave-reliefs, red on votive and architectural ones; and there was colour on the figures too. We possess no sculpture of this period on which much colour is preserved, but there are fine examples from the archaic Acropolis, buried after the Persian sack, and from the end of the fourth century the 'Alexander sarcophagus' preserved in a sealed tomb-chamber at Sidon. There is a world of difference between the schematic archaic colouring and the sophisticated pictorial treatment of the early Hellenistic reliefs, but they have this in common, and the Parthenon frieze will have had it with them: that the character of the marble is not obscured but glows through and harmonizes the colours. The effect is as different as can be from the plaster casts painted up in oils with which attempts are sometimes made to simulate what classical sculpture has lost in this respect.

The procession: representation and art

The Panathenaic procession formed up by one of the main gates in the city-wall of Athens, the Dipylon at the north-west. From about 400 B.C. there was a building, the Pompeion ('Procession-hall') immediately within the wall between the Dipylon and the closely neighbouring Sacred Gate from which the Sacred Way led out across Attica to the holy place of Eleusis. This building may have had a predecessor, but not necessarily, and the procession must in any case have been marshalled in the open. Once formed, it followed the Panathenaic Way through the city, across the Agora and up between the Areopagus and the west slope of the Acropolis, at the top of which was the entrance.

Of the procession shown on the Parthenon frieze, it is clear that the horsemen on the west face, and round the corner from the west on the north, are preparing. They are shown, that is, not in procession but as they might have been seen before they were ready to start, about the Dipylon Gate. Most of the horsemen up the long sides, and many of the other figures, are in movement towards the east, but the girls on the east face are again still. It is often suggested that these are thought of as already arrived on the Acropolis, while the two long sides show the procession in movement through the city from the preparation at the Dipylon shown on the west. This may be right; but there are things which tell against it. We know that men in armour leapt in and out of chariots as they moved in the procession, and some on the frieze are shown as doing this; but gesturing marshals move, sometimes violently, among them, checking and organizing, and where the horses are in motion the long-robed charioteers seem to be reining them in; while the last teams on both north and south, and on the south those at the head also, are perfectly still. Likewise the last of the four beautiful figures of youths with water-pots is stooping to lift his vessel off the ground and set it on his shoulder. Constantly one is brought back to stillness or unreadiness, and I wonder if the whole is not primarily intended to suggest a moment before the procession actually sets off.

There is a marked liking in classical art, especially in the phase just before this, for such an indirect approach to narrative, the choice of a moment before or after the climactic one. The east pediment at Olympia shows not the chariot-race between Oenomaus and Pelops, but still figures, their chariots quietly standing by, taking an oath to abide by its result. Two of Hercules' labours on the metopes of the same building are shown already accomplished, the exhausted boy standing on the body of the lion of Nemea, the grown man bringing the dead birds of Lake Stymphalus to Athena. So, Polygnotus' great mural at Delphi showed the old theme of the sack of Troy in a new guise: Troy taken; and in a temple at Plataea he painted Odysseus having slain the suitors. Not that one should try to pin such representations down to an exact moment. As the unities in Attic drama, at its height at this time, are only loosely observed, so there is elasticity in the conventions of this art. Neoptolemus in Polygnotus' Troy was still killing, while at the other end of the picture Greeks were taking down tents and preparing ships for departure; but we are left in no doubt that the tone of the picture was given by the great majority of still figures, the aftermath of the dreadful night. On the Parthenon frieze there are figures and groups, especially many of the horsemen, which are surely meant to suggest the procession as it looked on its way, but I see the overriding effect as one of preparation. The relaxed, informal attitudes not only of the figures between the procession and the gods but of the gods themselves fit with this; and the interpretation one chooses has an important bearing on the nature of the little scene at the centre, and with that on the question of what precisely one means by saying that the frieze represents the Panathenaic procession.

I have spoken of the frieze as illustrating an unlegendary activity, a ritual from contemporary life, but it has been strongly argued that what is shown is in fact legendary, though a unique choice from legend: the original procession, instituted by Erechtheus to honour the new-fallen image with a robe. Let us look more closely.

Most of the girls on the frieze carry ritual objects, but the pair in front at the south, the two pairs in front at the north, are empty-handed. The marshal facing the front pair at the north holds up something which they perhaps are to take from him, or have handed to him, but some at least of these surely have their hands free to carry the *peplos* at some stage of the ritual. If this is really the first procession, then there can only be one robe, the first, and that shown in the central scene must be it. The front of the procession must indeed have reached its bourne, the girls have handed over their precious burden; the culminating ceremony be taking place or about to take place. If that is so, however, the casual, gossipy air of the gods (their backs turned on this activity) and of the figures between them and the procession seems strange. Surely all these are waiting for the procession to pass, and the little scene at the centre is preparation too, those on the Acropolis making ready to receive the procession. The folded cloth will then be the *old* robe, its four-year service finished, implying the timeless repetition of the ritual.

If the procession shown on the frieze is not the original one, still less is it identifiable with that at any one Panathenaia of its own time. One need only compare it to another processional frieze carved in low relief four hundred years and more later, on parallel sides of the circuit-wall round the Ara Pacis Augustae, the Altar of Peace dedicated in Rome by Augustus in 9 B.C. The designer surely had the Parthenon frieze in mind, but idealized as his work is it contains unmistakable portraits and has been identified as representing the procession at the founding of the altar on 4 July 13 B.C. The frieze of the Parthenon gives us rather an ideal embodiment of a recurrent festival.

The two stools brought by the girls to the priestess in the central scene are often interpreted as symbolic invitations to the gods to be present. There was a festival of the Dioscuri known as the Theoxenia ('Gods as guests'), in which empty couches were set out, with loaded tables beside them, for the twin gods; and Apollo was honoured in the same way at some places and times. The Theoxenia of the Dioscuri was known in Athens in the fifth century, for it is shown on a few vases; but the parallel with the action on the frieze is not at all close, and the presence there, immediately abutting on this scene, of the twelve gods already seated does not help to make the explanation convincing. I like to think that the two stools are for the two robes, the old and the new, to be exposed side by side at some high point of the ceremony. There is no evidence that this occurred, but there is very little evidence indeed about the ritual.

We do not know where the image was kept at the time the Parthenon was built, nor where or in what manner the robe was delivered. A little later the image's home was the Erechtheum, and one striking feature of that strange building is perhaps of particular relevance here: the 'Maiden Porch'. This is a kind of loggia or verandah, projecting from the south wall and abutting directly on the foundations of the ancient temple which, until the Persian invasion, had housed the olive-wood idol. The entablature and ceiling of this projection are supported by Caryatids, colossal statues of girls serving as columns, which stand, four in front and two behind, on a continuous parapet which rises some five feet above the floor. The maidens seem to look straight across the old foundations to the Parthenon, and they markedly resemble the girls at the head of the procession on the frieze. Their hands are lost, but copies have come to light in Tivoli, made for Hadrian's Villa some two hundred years after the Ara Pacis. They are dull, chill work, but accurate and well-preserved, and each carries in one hand against her skirt a *phiale*, a shallow bowl for ritual libation, exactly as do some on both wings of the Parthenon procession. The 'porch' can never have been used as a normal entrance. Its only access from outside is a narrow breach in the parapet at the back of one side, behind the Caryatid, and it is joined to the interior by a narrow stair down to a room at a lower level which has its main entrance at the north. One might rather think this loggia designed for the enactment of some ritual, the performers in which would be protected and in a considerable degree concealed by the parapet, but could display above it that part of their mystery which the waiting crowd might have a part in. With its reminiscences of the Parthenon procession, it is tempting to see in it the setting for a culminating rite with robes and image.

Subsequent history

The Parthenon was finished just before the outbreak of the Peloponnesian War in 431 B.C., which seems to have interrupted work on the lovely entrance-complex of the Acropolis, the Propylaea. This was never completed, but probably late in the first phase of the war, before the Peace of Nicias in 421, the little temple of Athena Nike outside the gate was built. The Erechtheum seems to have been begun immediately after the peace, but work dragged on and it was hardly finished before Athens' final and crushing defeat in 404 B.C. No important building was done on the Acropolis after this, but in the early fourth century the city recovered her prosperity and she was one of the leaders in resisting the Macedonian aggression, which was building up during the middle decades of the century. Philip of Macedon triumphed at Chaeronea a century after the dedication of the Parthenos, and thereafter Athens only enjoyed brief and largely illusory periods of independence, being generally subject during the next two hundred years to one or other of the Hellenistic monarchies, and after that to Rome. Civic and religious life, however, seems to have gone on much on the old pattern. The gold was stripped from the Parthenos by a dictator at the beginning of the third century, but it was later replaced, and the city began to live on the past, her cultural heritage being admired and patronized by the kings of Pergamum, Syria and Egypt. She espoused the cause of Mithridates of Pontus, who sought to drive the Romans out of the east Mediterranean, and fell with him in 88 B.C., suffering a savage sack by the Roman general Sulla. Again the city revived, enjoying a final phase as a university town and tourist centre under the Roman empire. During all these changes the Panathenaic festival continued to be celebrated. It is uncertain how much the Acropolis with its buildings suffered from the devastations of Sulla's troops, and again in the ruin that fell on the lower city at the irruption of the barbarian Herulians during the troubles of the empire in the later third century A.D. By then, however, Athens was going into real decline, and the triumph of Christianity did her no good. In 391 Theodosius banned all pagan cults throughout the empire and closed the temples, and in 529 Justinian shut down the Schools of Athens.

At some uncertain date, probably later in the sixth century, the Parthenon was converted into a church. The orientation was reversed and a doorway opened between the two chambers, so that the west porch became the entrance to the whole building. An apse was thrown out at the east, and in the course of this operation the centre of the west pediment collapsed and the figures were lost. This was probably not deliberate; at least the central slab of the east frieze, which had to be removed in the construction of the apse, was taken down carefully and preserved intact. The heads on it have suffered deliberate defacement, but that was probably done at some later time; being for centuries at ground-level it was vulnerable. At some stage some deliberate mutilation was inflicted on some of the metopes, but the west pediment and the rest of the frieze (apart from the cutting of some windows) were left untouched and it is clear that there was no consistent policy of iconoclasm. The fact that the building continued in use and repair, moreover, meant that the condition of the sculptures remained relatively good through the long twilight of Byzantium, when Athens dwindled to a village in a neglected province, frequently subject to barbarian irruption from north or west. After the Turkish conquest in the late fifteenth century, the church was converted to a mosque, but the fortunes of the place did not much change. The Acropolis, however, remained a fortress of some importance, and during a siege by Venetian forces in 1687 the Turks stored their powder in the Parthenon. One of Morosini's gunners succeeded in firing it, and the whole centre of the building was blown out. The central metopes and a tract of the frieze on each side were destroyed, though fragments survive. The citadel surrendered and Morosini caused further loss by an unsuccessful attempt to remove figures from the west pediment.

The place was recovered by the Turks not long after. A small mosque was built in the ruins, but no attempt was made to restore or preserve the building, and both fabric and sculpture began to deteriorate rapidly through the ravages of nature and man. Observation of these conditions led Lord Elgin, who came in 1799 intending only to draw and take casts of the sculpture, to change his plan, and he contrived to purchase a large part of the carvings and remove them to London. What he took includes the greater part of the frieze, but the west face except for the return of the last slab of the north frieze and the slab next to it, remains on the building, where it has since suffered considerably as comparison with casts taken by Elgin shows. Many slabs which had fallen and become buried were only excavated later and are now in the Acropolis Museum. One such, from the east end, had been found in the 1780s and been bought by the French Ambassador to the Porte, the Duc de Choiseul-Gouffier. It is now in the Louvre, and there are fragments in other collections.

For about fifty years after the expulsion of the Turks from Athens in 1833, clearance of the crowded dwellings on the Acropolis and excavation of the silted site went on in rather a haphazard manner, but in the 1880s a regular and thorough programme was carried through by the Archaeological Society of Athens. The re-erection of the columns and entablature of the Parthenon thrown down by the explosion belongs largely to this century. In the course of excavation many fragments of the Parthenon sculptures were found, including some twenty-five slabs, or substantial parts of slabs, from the frieze. These are now exhibited in the Acropolis Museum.

The shipping of the Elgin marbles to London was a long and hazardous process. It began late in 1801, small vessels taking them to Alexandria, where they were transferred to larger craft. In September 1802, a ship-load went down off Cerigo (Kythera), south of the Peloponnese. The seventeen cases were salvaged, but the process, and their forwarding via Malta, with Nelson's help, to London, took four years. Most of the sculptures had reached England by 1804, but forty cases were still in Greece in 1807, when war broke out between England and Turkey, and did not arrive till 1811. The first exhibition was opened in 1807, and the enthusiastic reception encouraged Elgin to hope to sell the marbles, on the purchase and transfer of which he had spent a very large sum, to the nation. Negotiations were opened in 1810, and after prolonged discussions and the report of a Select Committee in 1815, they were purchased for £35,000, less than half what Elgin was hoping for. They were exhibited in the British Museum in 1817, in temporary accommodation, and a permanent gallery was opened in 1831. A century later a new gallery was offered by Lord Duveen. This was completed in 1939, but suffered damage during the war, and the marbles were not placed in it and opened to exhibition until 1961. It is there that the greater part of the frieze is now to be seen.

The influence of the frieze

No other Greek temple, so far as we can see, is adorned with a representation of a religious ceremony. In this respect the innovation of the Parthenon frieze seems to have remained unique. On almost all other temples the representations continue to be taken from the old store of myth and legend, and it is noteworthy that the exceptions or doubtful cases are to be found among temples built in Athens in the time of the Parthenon itself or shortly afterwards. The east frieze of the temple of Hephaestus above the Agora has an obscure but certainly mythological subject: a battle, interrupted by two groups of seated deities. There must be some connection between this design and that of the east frieze of the Parthenon, but the two buildings were under construction at the same time and there is no saying how the influence went. Equally obscure are the subjects of the scattered slabs from the frieze of a little Ionic temple built beside the Ilissus in the Periclean age and destroyed by the Turks in the eighteenth century, but these again are narrative episodes, seemingly mythological. The east frieze of the closely related but still smaller temple of Athena Nike, built outside the Propylaea probably as we saw towards the end of the first phase of the Peloponnesian war, is no less difficult to interpret. This recurrent obscurity in Athenian religious art of this period is interesting and curious, but the quiet groups of this frieze do not seem to be engaged in any ritual or ceremony comparable to the Panathenaic procession. The other three friezes of this building show battles, that on the south a battle of Greeks against opponents in Persian dress. It seems certain that this is a direct representation of the Persian wars, and good arguments have been adduced to show that Marathon is specifically intended. This then is a case of the carving on a temple of mortal activity from near-contemporary life – people who remembered Marathon must have been living in Athens when the frieze was carved. It thus goes beyond the Parthenon frieze in that it is not, like that, the ideal image of a recurrent religious activity, but a representation of a single, precise occurrence. The Persian wars, however, and particularly, for the Athenians, Marathon, had attained much of the status of heroic legend. A suggestion that the north and west friezes, where the fighters are not distinguished, might show fifth-century battles of Greek against Greek seems to me quite impossible; or at least I feel that it would require very much harder evidence than this to show that such a thing would be possible in the decoration of a temple. I would suppose that here the Persian wars are lifted into the company of legendary conflicts, perhaps those of Athens under her early kings against her neighbours.

All these friezes are much smaller than that of the Parthenon and show little or no formal influence from it. The parapet set round the bastion of the Nike temple, with Victories variously engaged, interspersed with seated figures of Athena, is nearer the Parthenon frieze in scale. Groups with sacrificial cattle echo a theme from it, but the style of the figures is as different as the character of the relief. One class of relief-sculpture in later fifth-century Athens, however, does show direct inspiration from the style of the frieze: the marble gravestones. There is a splendid series of figured tombstones from sixth-century Attica, but they seem to have been only for the aristocratic and the rich and they come to an abrupt end about the time of the establishment of the democracy. A law may perhaps have been passed restricting funeral expenditure, such as we know put an end in 317 or a year or two later to the series which begins in Pericles' time. This series differs sharply from the archaic in its social range. Sosinus on a stone in the Louvre, Xanthippus on one in the British Museum, sit like the gods of the frieze, but Xanthippus holds a cobbler's last and Sosinus a pair of bellows. Sosinus is described in an epitaph as a bronze-worker from Cretan Gortyn; he was a metic, that is. Xanthippus' name appears alone, without that of his father or other description. This suggests that he was a slave; surely a slave, as her cropped hair shows, was the girl Mynno who sits spinning on a charming small stone in Berlin; while others are shown with certainty to have been citizens or citizens' wives.

The very striking resemblance of some of these figures to figures on the frieze, and the sudden new flourishing of this art at this time, are surely to be explained by the fact that completion of work on the Parthenon sculpture released a large body of finely trained craftsmen, some of whom found this new employment. Few of these stones are masterpieces or suggest the design of a great artist. They are excellent work by skilful journeymen; men, in their different occupation, like Sosinus and Xanthippus, and like those whose names appear in the inscription recording payments for the execution of the friezes of the Erechtheum. A similar range of social background is witnessed in the inscriptions set by dedicators on marble reliefs which are now offered to the Nymphs and Pan, to Asklepios (Aesculapius, god of healing) and his family, and to other popular deities and demigods, hitherto recipients of humbler gifts. All this seems to show that the great works on the Acropolis had a truly wide appeal. Athenian democracy was founded on more than one gross injustice and committed many more, but within its limits the spread of light was real.

Direct influence from the style of the frieze naturally faded out in a generation or two, as sculptors developed their art in different ways, but we meet a revival of it from time to time in later centuries. We noticed that Hellenistic Athens was patronized by the kings of Pergamum, and the sculptors who worked for the Pergamene court were steeped in Periclean art. A copy of the Parthenos and its base stood in the library there; and even the reliefs of the huge frieze round the great altar of Zeus, for whose style it is impossible not to borrow the word baroque, show on analysis constant echoes of the art of the Parthenon. Most of the clearest borrowings and echoes are from the pediments, whose scale and character render them more suitable to adaptation in this context; but a long-robed deity driving a chariot against a Giant is far too like for chance to a group of chariot and marshal from the north frieze, though transformed by scale, the character of the relief, and the style of the time into something very different.

Nearly two centuries later again, we noticed the designer of Augustus' Ara Pacis looking to the frieze for inspiration. Later in the empire one might perhaps trace its influence in Hadrian's classicizing revival of the mid second century; certainly there are direct imitations of pediment-figures in Hadrianic and Antonine art; but after that it would be hard I think to detect it for nearly a millennium and a half. Cyriac of Ancona travelled in Greece in the fifteenth century, and drew among other things the Parthenon, and copies of his drawings circulated widely in Italy; but neither he nor his copyists were in sympathy with Periclean art. A little later the sympathy was there, but by then contacts were less good. The Adam of the Sistine ceiling is astonishingly like some figures from the Parthenon pediments, but there is no question of direct influence; and it might be difficult to find even indirect influence from the frieze.

In the second half of the seventeenth century, before the explosion of 1687, a French ambassador to the Porte took a draughtsman to Athens. There is some confusion about his identity: one person who knew him refers to him as a Fleming, but he was more probably a Frenchman, Jacques Carrey of Troyes. His principal commission was to draw the sculptures of the Parthenon. He has left us records of both pediments as they existed in his day (the east not very different from what we have, but there was far more in the west), and the metopes of the south side, including the now perished ones in the centre. Of the frieze, we have his records of the east and west fronts complete, the easternmost third of the north, and about a third from the middle of the south. The metopes on east, north, and west were already very much defaced, and he probably deliberately omitted them, but there is good reason to think that originally he drew the whole of the frieze. The loss is sad, for what remains includes only a part of the areas destroyed in the explosion and later, and these are drawings of real value. We noticed that the 'baroque' sculptors of Hellenistic Pergamon show an appreciation of the art of the Parthenon; and it is remarkable that these seventeenth-century drawings reveal much more feeling for the character of the sculptures than others produced in the late eighteenth and early nineteenth centuries. Those are the work of classicizing artists, who believed themselves returning from the corruption of baroque to the pure style of the fifth century. Their conscious classicism seems to have come between them and the originals, and their drawings strike a chill. The earlier artist drew much more directly what he saw, and a spark of the original spirit is caught in his work.

Nevertheless, the influence of the Elgin marbles in the early nineteenth century was profound. The exhibition in London in 1807 was the first occasion on which a body of great original Greek sculpture was seen in western Europe, and it was a revelation to art-lovers and artists alike. This is witnessed in the report of the Select Committee and in the comments of Canova (who lamented that he could not unlearn all he had learned and start again), Flaxman, Haydon, and many others; and the influence extended beyond the visual arts. To Haydon's introduction of Keats to the marbles we owe not only the sonnets on them – 'these wonders' – but certainly also the Ode on a Grecian Urn, which (though the genesis of the 'urn' is a complex question) undoubtedly takes much of its imagery directly from the frieze.

Phidias and the Parthenon

The sculptures of the Parthenon, and perhaps particularly the frieze, are often thought of as showing the style of Phidias. How far is this justified? Direct evidence for that artist's participation in the work is, as many scholars have emphasized, quite lacking; yet the popular opinion may well be right.

Plutarch tells us that Phidias acted as general overseer of Pericles' work on the Acropolis, and though Plutarch was writing more than half a millennium later he used older authorities, often good ones. This seems a case where there is no reason whatever to doubt the truth of his assertion. There is plentiful and varied evidence that Phidias was a member of the Periclean circle and a victim of indirect attacks on the statesman by his political enemies. If we are right about the nature of the representation on the frieze, its sharp break with the traditions of religious art is exactly the kind of thing which those enemies used to discredit Pericles and his friends with the more conservative sections of the Athenian public.

More significant than these general considerations is the close relation we noticed between Parthenos and Parthenon. Statue and temple were created at the same time, and the building was in a special sense a shrine, a setting for the image. The notable correspondences which exist between the subsidiary adornment of the one and the other surely mean that the artist of the statue had some direct say in the programme of the sculptural decoration for the building. It does not follow from this that Phidias gave any detailed designs for the sculpture. The creation of the statue must have been an enormous labour, and there were other good sculptors in Athens, whose names are associated with Phidias' in the records: Agoracritus of Paros for one; Alcamenes another. Nevertheless, the possibility of Phidias' direct participation remains.

The overall design for each pediment must have been given in some detail by one artist; but though the two designs are certainly related the same man need not necessarily have given both. Moreover, each pediment-figure (or in some cases two figures carved from one block) while fitting perfectly within a closely knit composition, is designed and executed as a statue existing in its own right; and one could imagine the detailed designing of these being parcelled out among several artists.

The metopes, except those of the Centauromachy, and a lovely one with two goddesses from the east end of the north side, are not in a condition to allow any judgement of this kind to be hazarded about them. Those which are well preserved differ among themselves in character and quality more than any other part of the sculptures. They appear to have been carved earliest, at a time before the team of executants had been trained and weeded out; and one might guess that the craftsmen were in some cases working from designs of a more summary kind than were provided for the pediments and frieze.

The frieze is different again. The treatment of relief is unique and highly individual, and it is adhered to with great consistency through all the variety of subject-matter and grouping; and this seems to me only one aspect of a profound harmony and unity. I would suppose it likely that one artist had supplied a detailed design for the whole. Even if this is so, one cannot assert that the artist was Phidias. Nevertheless, the record is clear that Phidias was the greatest and most influential figure in the art of his time. The purest distillation of that art to survive for us is the Parthenon frieze, and if we read it as Phidian we cannot be altogether wrong.

Bibliography

A. H. SMITH *The Sculptures of the Parthenon* London, 1910
Basically a catalogue of the material in the British Museum, this is the only attempt at full publication of the scattered sculptures, using early drawings and casts and assembling a large number of fragments. It is, however, very imperfect.

G. FOUGÈRES *L'Acropole d'Athènes 2, Le Parthénon* Paris, 1910
Plates illustrating the building and its sculptures, with brief introduction.

M. COLLIGNON *Le Parthénon. L'Histoire, l'Architecture et la Sculpture* Paris, 1912
The plates of the last with a much fuller text. The text was reissued under the same title in 1914, with much reduced illustration and in a smaller format.

P. E. CORBETT *The Sculpture of the Parthenon* Harmondsworth, 1959
The best general account.

D. E. L. HAYNES *The Parthenon Frieze* London, n.d. (1959)
A selection of photographs with a sensitive introductory essay.

Parthenos and Parthenon (supplement to *Greece and Rome*, Oxford, 1963)
Essays by various hands on various aspects; particularly valuable, Alison Burford on 'The builders of the Parthenon' and Russell Meiggs on 'The political implications of the Parthenon'. The section on the sculptures, by the present writer, has a fairly full bibliography to date.

F. BROMMER *Die Skulpturen der Parthenongiebel* Mainz, 1963, and *Die Metopen des Parthenon* Mainz, 1967
These two books are complete catalogues, with very full, thorough and scholarly discussions, of respectively the pediments and the metopes. A companion book of the same kind on the frieze is promised by the same scholar and is eagerly awaited.

RHYS CARPENTER *The Architects of the Parthenon* Harmondsworth, 1970
This controversial book is mentioned in the text.

T. BOWIE and D. THIMME *The Carrey Drawings of the Parthenon Sculpture* Indiana University Press, Bloomington and London, 1971
A full publication of the Carrey drawings, with photographs of the corresponding originals where they survive, and a historical account.

B. ASHMOLE *Architect and Sculptor in Classical Greece*
Phaidon Press, London, and New York University Press, 1972
Contains a sensitive and illuminating discussion of the Parthenon and its sculptures (including an important section on the frieze), with a special interest in the practical problems involved in the realization of this grand conception.

1–3 The photograph at the top shows the west face of the temple now. The dark interior of the building behind the colonnade was reached through the six-columned inner porch. The west frieze is *in situ* above those columns (left). Parts of the central slabs (West VII and VIII; one block below restored) are shown right. At frieze-level on the outside the metopes (separated by triglyphs) are carved with combats, of Greek and Amazon probably, but they are very much defaced. Of the statues in the pediment, which showed the strife of Athena and Poseidon, only the group known as Cecrops and his daughter is now in place. Above the apex of the cornice was a floral akroterion.

1 1 2 3 4 II 5

SOUTH

Note

The identification of the slabs along each side by Roman numerals, and of the figures on them by Arabic, goes back to a publication by Adolf Michaelis, *Der Parthenon* (Leipzig 1871), with slight adjustments by Smith in the publication listed in the bibliography. The only substantial rearrangement is of the remains of slabs XXXVIII–XLIII at the end of the south side; see the note there. The slabs numbered East I and IX (this one lost but recorded in drawings) and West I and XVI are not in fact separate slabs but the short return-ends of respectively South XLIV and North I (lost but recorded) and North XLII and South I.

All the surviving slabs are in the British Museum, except the following: Athens, Acropolis, *in situ* on the Parthenon: South I and IV (mainly; there are fragments of both in London); West III–XVI.
Athens, Acropolis Museum: South XIV, XVI–XVIII; also fragments of XIX–XXI, XXIII–XXIV, XXVI, XXIX, XXXII, XXXIV–VI, XLIII and XLIV; East I (small fragment), II (surviving part), VI (38–40; 41–7 lost but recorded in casts); North II, III (fragments), IV, VI, fragments of VIII–IX, X, fragments of XI–XIII, fragments of XV–XVII, fragments of XIX–XXII, fragments of XXIV, fragment of XXVII, XXIX, XXX (surviving part), XXXI.
Paris, Louvre: East VII; head of youth of uncertain place.
Vienna, Kunsthistorisches Museum: fragment of North IX.
Palermo: East VI 40 (small fragment, feet).
There are other fragments of uncertain placing in Athens and London.

IV 10 11 V 12 13 14

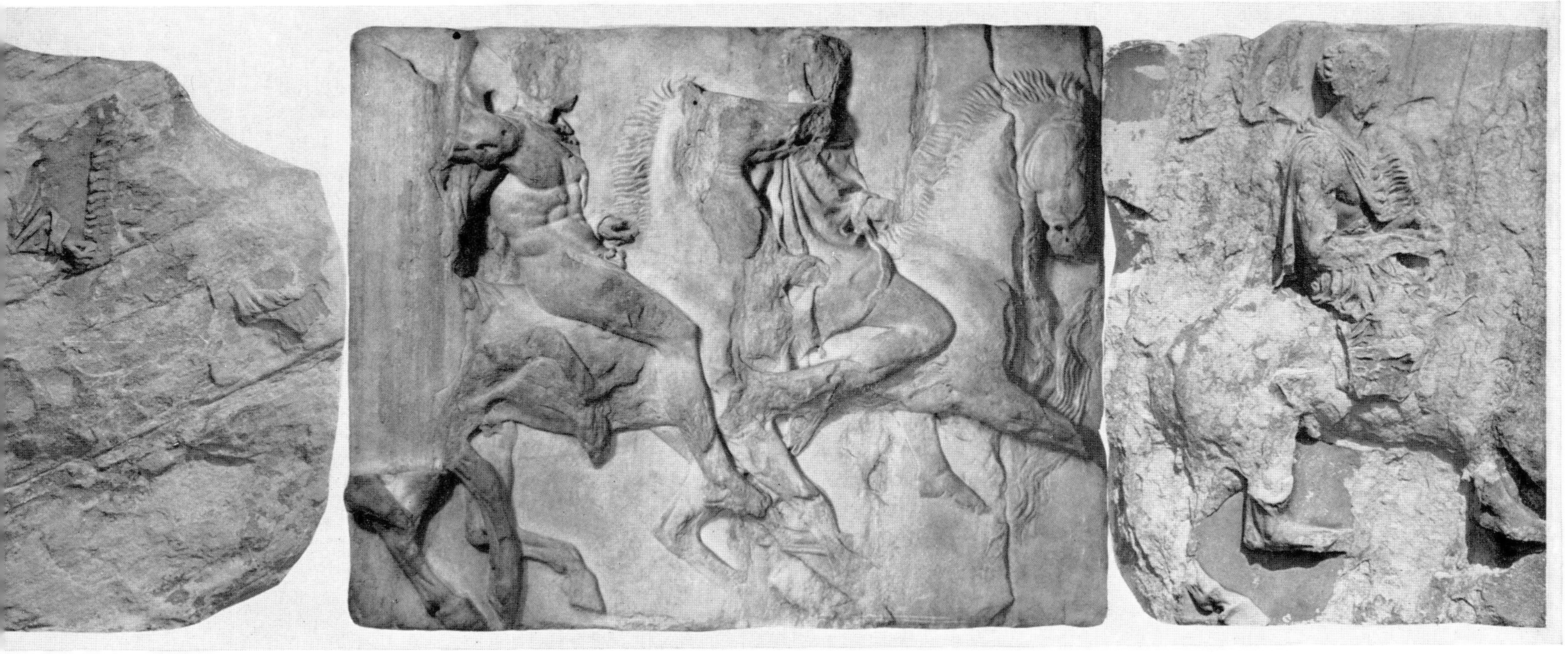

6 7 III 8 9 IV 10

The Frieze

We begin with the south frieze, taking the procession from the rear to its culmination on the east end of the building; then back again, surveying the north side from east to west. The rear of the procession on both north and south is taken up by Knights, and the west end of the building shows them preparing themselves and their mounts. The general movement across the west is from south to north, and the north frieze follows straight out of it, so we will take the west face at the end.

The south frieze has suffered very badly from weathering, much of the surface of many slabs having split away, and the cortège can in general be better appreciated on the north.

The Knights were one of the ancient classes of Attic society, and their existence was recognized in Solon's codification of the laws. The Greek word (*hippeis*) means simply 'horsemen', and originally perhaps defined the class of those who could afford to supply themselves with a mount in their military service for the state. By the time of the Parthenon, however, the Knights were a cavalry corps of rich young aristocrats, which was part of the army and also figured prominently in the contests and processions accompanying religious festivals. These it is who bring up the rear of the procession shown on the Parthenon.

Many pictures on Attic vases of the earlier fifth century illustrate the *dokimasia*, the inspection of the young men and their mounts, which they had to pass before being admitted to the corps of Knights. The youths in these pictures sport a great variety of wear: most have cloaks, but while some favour skin caps with lappets, others wear wide-brimmed hats, yet others are bare-headed; and while some wear a tunic under the cloak others are naked. All these styles recur among the riders on the frieze, some of whom are cuirassed and helmeted as though for war;

VI 15 16 VII 17 18 19 20

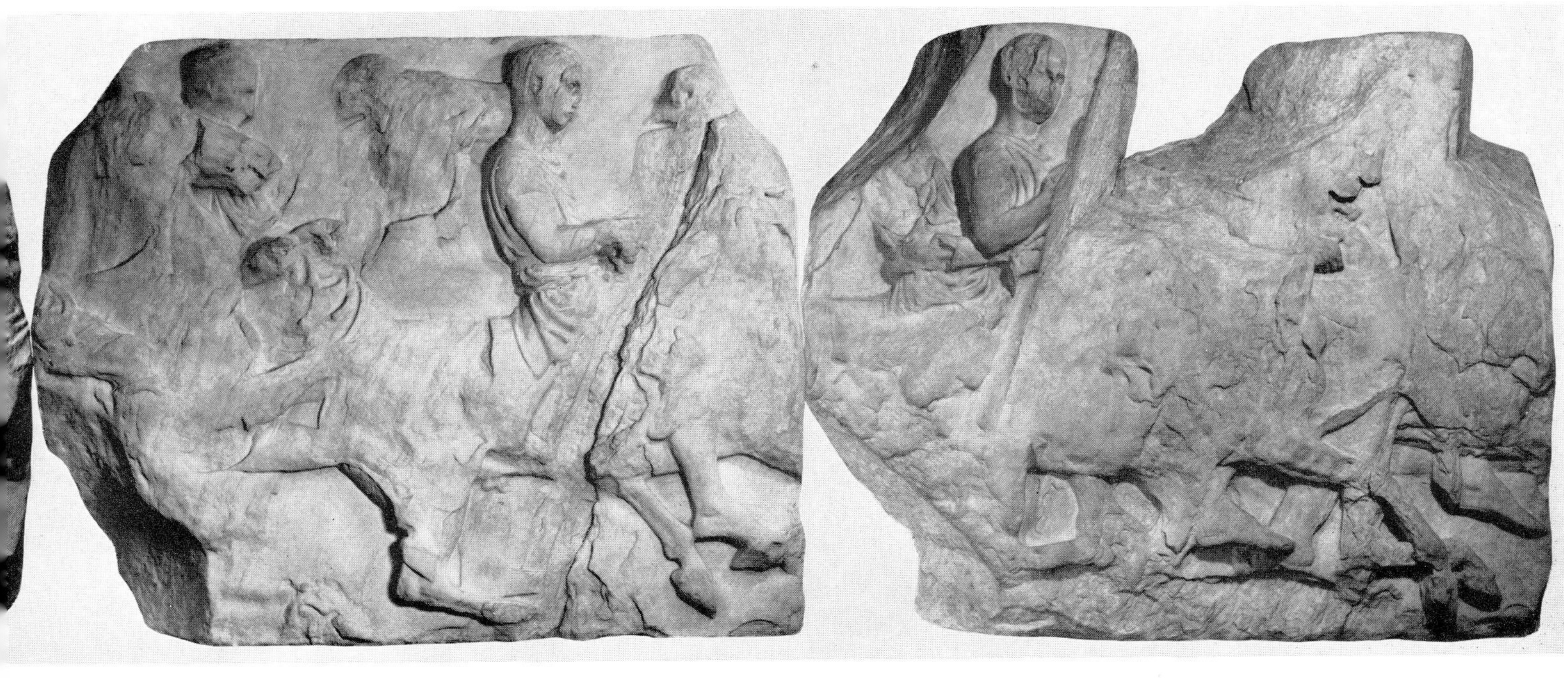

VIII 21 22 23 IX 24 25 X

SOUTH

and they may be barefoot, sandalled or booted. All these features are better seen on the north and west. This variety no doubt reflects actual practice; but it is unlikely that young men rode naked in Athenian processions, and when they are shown so it is surely by artistic licence.

Another convention in defiance of nature is noticeable in these groups: the relative proportions of men and horses. The figures on foot in the frieze are of a size to occupy nearly the height of the slab. Most of the riders if dismounted, would come little short of the same height; and the horses, when they are shown in stillness (as on West XV) stand about head high to man. Next to men Greek artists loved horses, and those of the frieze are superb; but Man is what Greek art is about, and everything else is subordinated to him.

Greek horses were indeed probably small by modern standards, but other representations make it evident that they were larger in proportion to their riders than those on the frieze appear. What breed is shown is a question sometimes canvassed but never answered with any certainty. The Greeks themselves distinguished different breeds, or at least horses from different localities with different characteristics, but to equate the written accounts with the monuments appears impossible. The horse seems to have been introduced into the lands around the Mediterranean in the second millennium B.C., and all horses known to the Greeks will have been descended from this basic stock. Differences in their representation probably have more to do with changes in artistic climate than with the stud. The later sixth century was in part an age of elegance, and the marble horses dedicated then on the Acropolis are as fine-boned and delicate-stepping as the *korai*, the marble girls with their elaborate clothes and hair-dos, among whom they stood. In the time of the Persian Wars comes reaction, the 'severe style', when the smile fades from the faces of the athletes and the upstanding women, their heavy robes falling in columnar folds. The still, massive horses from the east gable of the temple of Zeus at Olympia are fit creatures to draw such figures. In the horses, as in the human and divine figures, of the Parthenon, vivid observation and charm return without loss of classical gravity.

XII 32 33 34 XIII 35 36 37

26 27 28 XI 29 30 31 XII

XIV 38 39 XV 40 41 XVI

XVI 42 43 XVII 44 45 XV

SOUTH

The riders go bareback, with neither saddle nor cloth, stirrup nor spur. This is always so in Greek representations, and it is probable that none of these things was at this time and place in use. Stirrups, indeed, we know were an invention of the middle ages. Evidence for the spur does go back in Greece to a time not much after the Parthenon, but it was probably only then invented or introduced. The saddle is much older in some forms and some places, but seems not to have been used for riding in classical Greece. Some sixth-century vase-paintings from east of the Aegean show a cloth laid across the back of a ridden horse, and the custom was common in the Assyrian and after that in the Persian empire, but it does not seem to have spread to mainland Greece. A donkey with a timber-framed pack-saddle is shown on an Athenian vase of half a century earlier than the Parthenon, but of the riding-saddle with a rigid tree there is no trace. Riders are sometimes shown carrying a short stick to beat the animal's flanks, and it is possible that such were added in bronze or paint for some figures on the frieze. Bit and rein were certainly so shown; adjuncts of bronze were freely used throughout the frieze, though now only drill-holes remain to show where they were set. There were many types of bit in use in classical Greece, both for ridden and draught horses.

XX 49 50 XXI 51 52 53 XXII

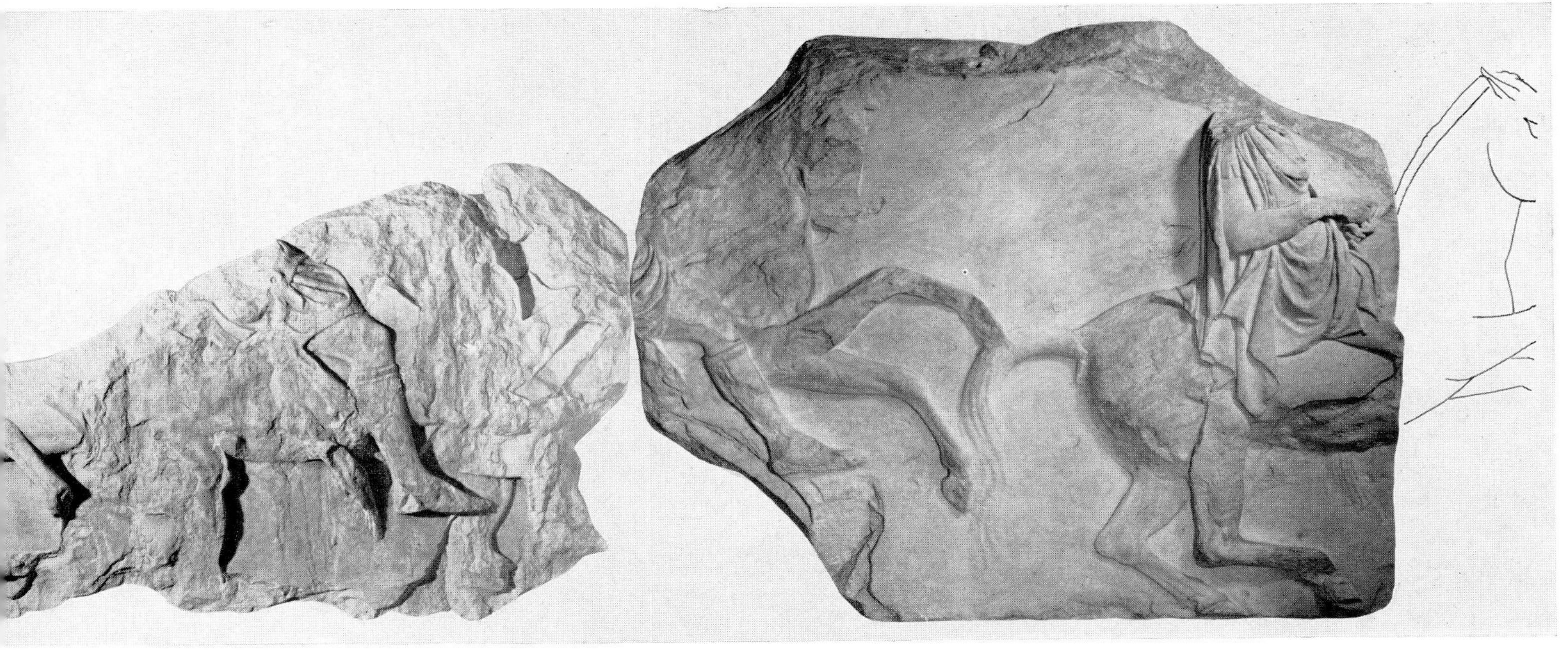

46 XIX 47 48 XX

54 55 56 XXIII 57 58

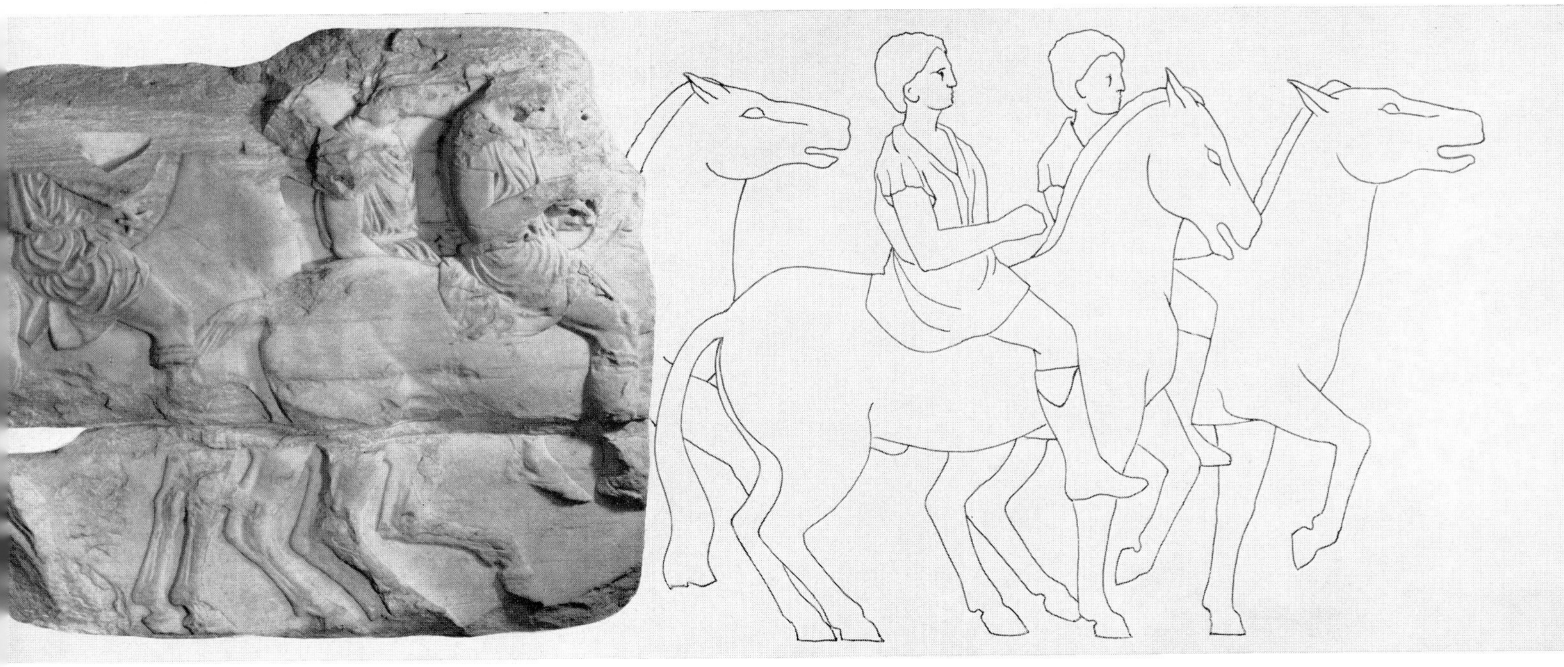

XXIV 59 60 XXV 61 62 63

SOUTH

In front of the horsemen are shown chariots (xxiv-xxxiv), but here we come, on both south and north, to the area of the frieze most severely damaged in the explosion of 1687, which blew out the middle of the building. The losses on the south side are recorded in Carrey's drawings. Again we can best appreciate these groups on the north, though that is very fragmentary too and there are still beautiful figures on the south: as the man standing quietly by the still team (xxv 61), or the one in a moving chariot turning to look back (xxx 74).

The four-horse chariot is a weapon of war in Homer, though mainly as a means of conveying a warrior to the battle or about the field, setting him down to fight and picking him up again; actual fighting from a chariot seldom takes place. Whether the heroic four-in-hand is a reminiscence of earlier practice or a poetic extravagance, the chariots and carts shown on eighth- and seventh-century vases (of the time when the Homeric epics took shape) are normally drawn by only two horses. In the sixth century the four-horse chariot becomes common in scenes from heroic mythology; and when, about the middle of the century, Panathenaic prize-vases begin to carry pictures of the events in the games, four-horse chariots appear on them. It is probably safe to assume that the four-horse chariot-race was already a feature of the older and greater games at Olympia and Delphi.

In historical times this race was the most conspicuous event of the great games. Only the very wealthy could put in teams, and victory, especially at Olympia, carried great prestige and was much sought after. This is witnessed, a generation before the Parthenon, in Pindar's odes, in particular some of those for the tyrants of the cities of Sicily; and a generation after in stories about Alcibiades. In the race, the rich and great did not mount their own chariots, which only carried a lightly clad driver; nor were chariots ever used by Greeks of historical times in war. The pictures from heroic mythology, following the text of Homer, show the war-chariot driven by an unarmed charioteer and carrying as passenger the fully-armed hero. What is shown on the Parthenon frieze is a kind of game based on this image. There was a foot-race in armour in which the competitor (*hoplitodromos*) was not

XXIX 71 72 XXX 73 74

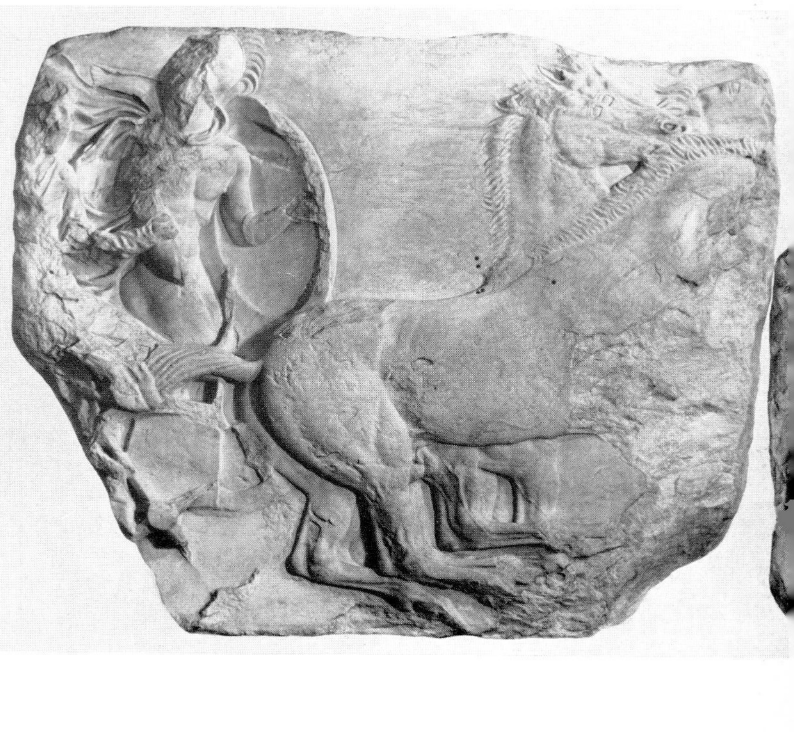

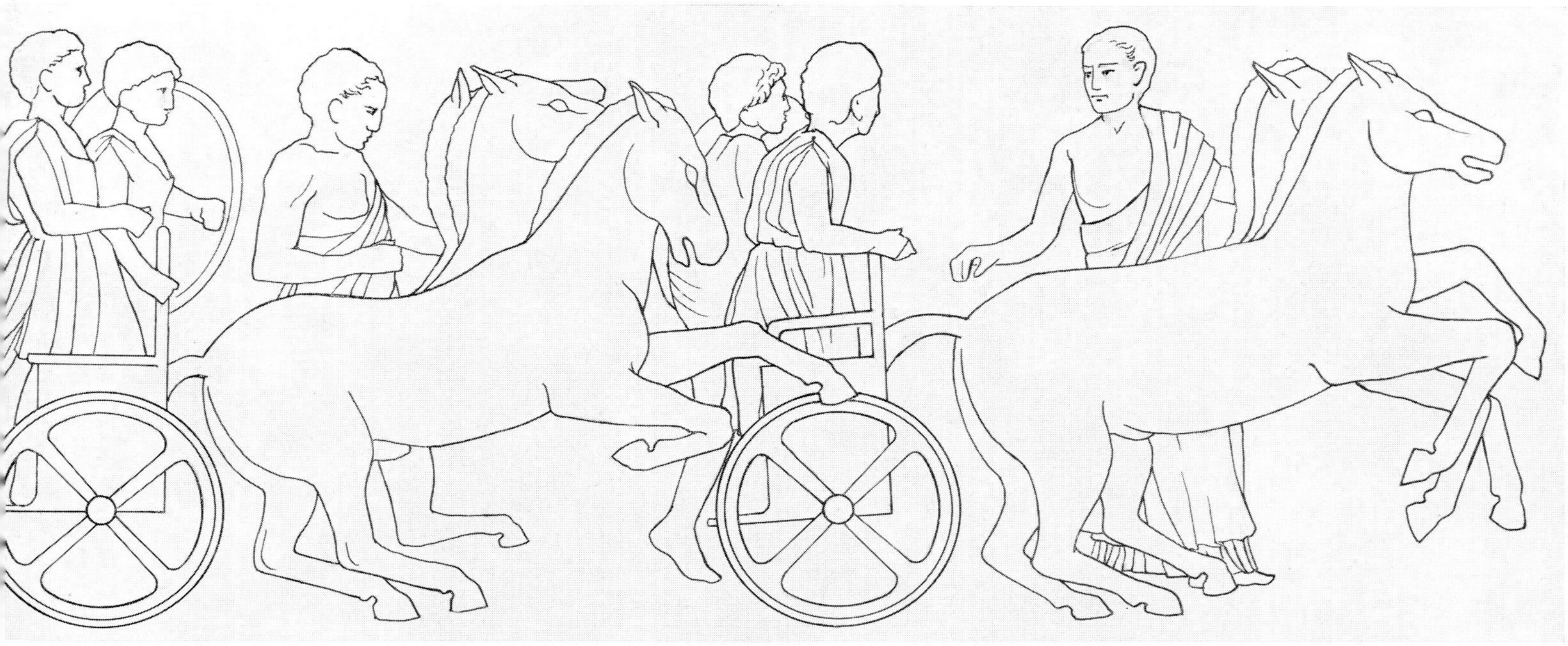

XXVI 64 65 66 XXVII 67 68 69 (XXVIII 70)

fully armed but wore a helmet and carried the heavy, round infantry shield. In the chariot-contest the team was driven by a lightly clad charioteer, and the *apobates* (literally 'dismounter'), with helmet and shield, leaped in and out of the car as it moved at speed. There are further representations of the event on small reliefs of rather later date dedicated for victories. These men belong, like the mounted Knights behind them, to the rich and aristocratic section of Athenian society. Here too some are shown tunicked, some naked.

XI 75 76 77 XXXII 78 79 80

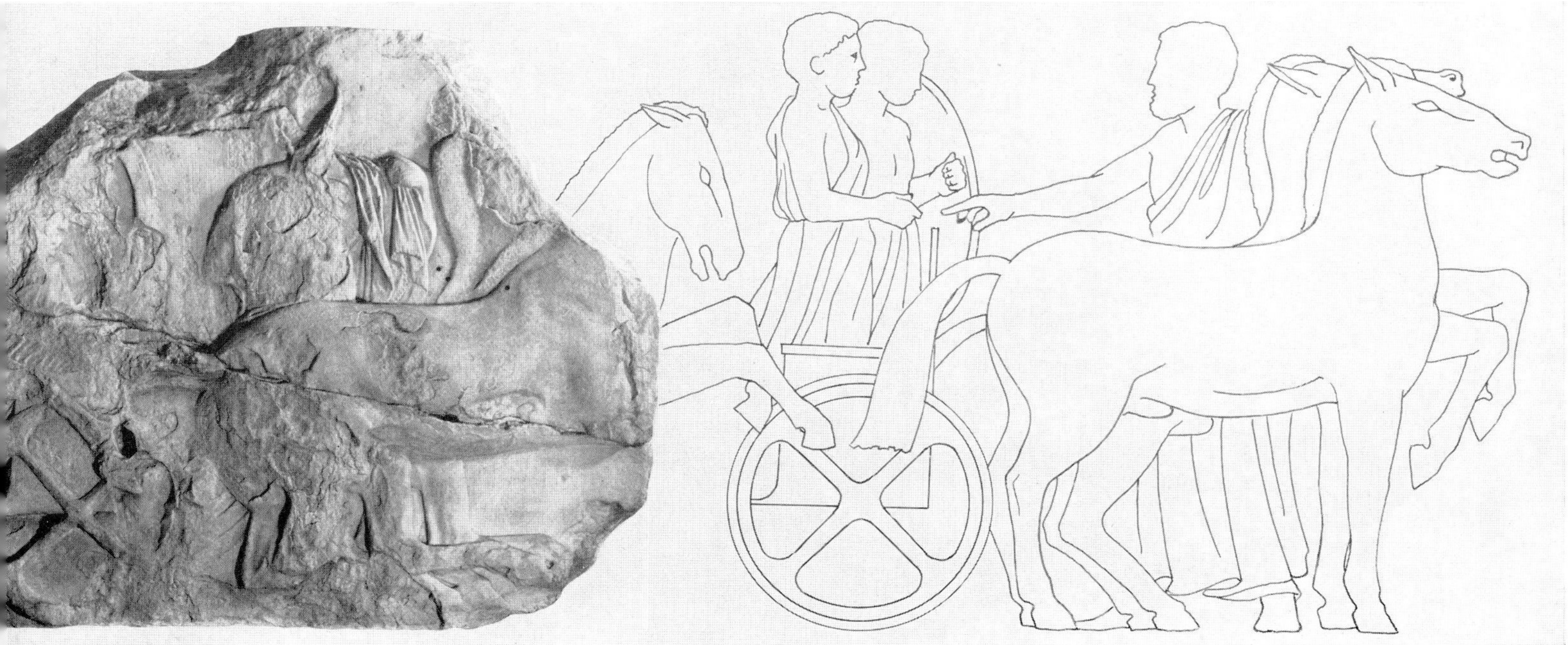

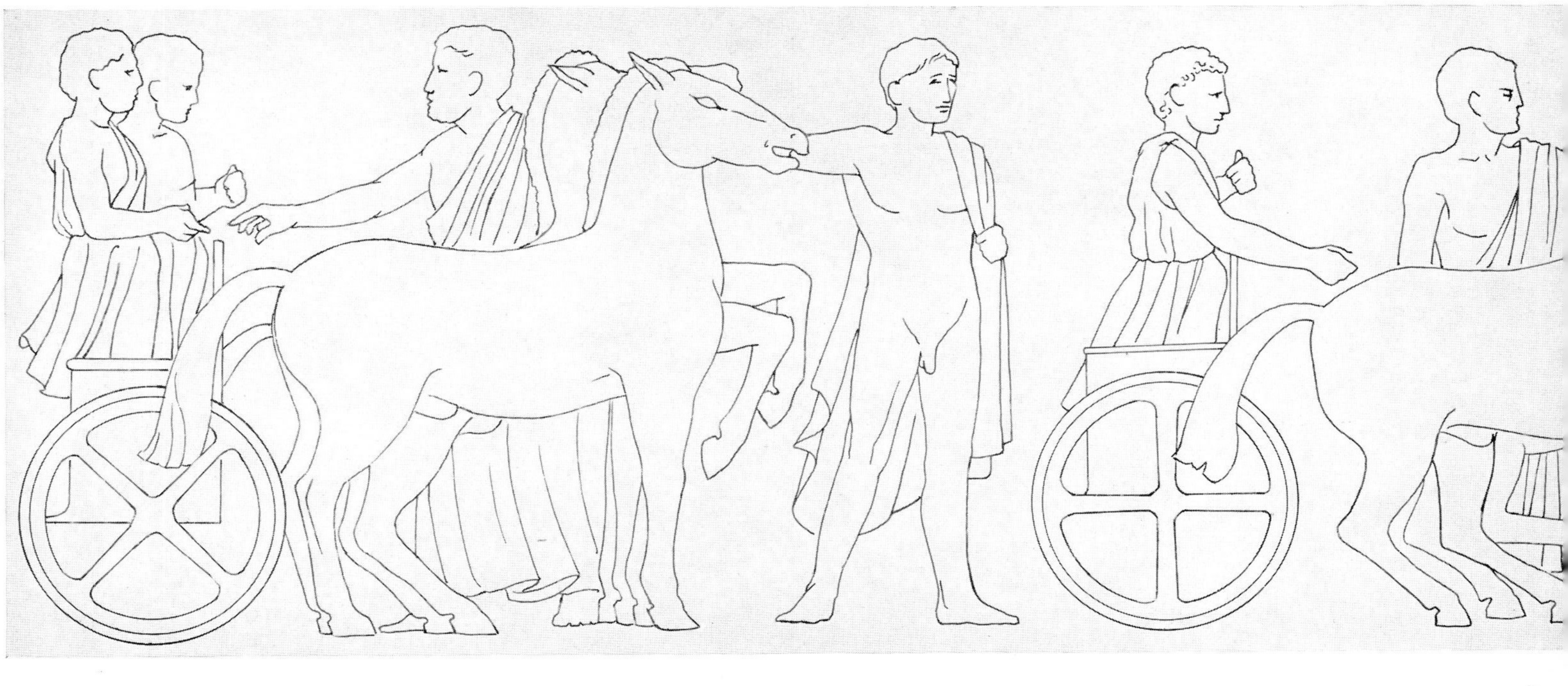

XXXII SOUTH 78 79 80 XXXIII 81 82 83

In front of the chariots comes a group of elders (XXXIV–XXXVI), walking and talking together. This stretch was even more horribly ravaged by the explosion than that with the chariots. One slab on the north is tolerably preserved, but on the south we have to depend on Carrey's drawings to place the sad fragments in the composition. He seems to have taken the figures in front of the elders (XXXVII) for women, which is almost certainly wrong. Those on the corresponding slabs on the north are men playing lyres and pipes, and in front of them others carrying ritual objects. The objects carried by 102–4 in Carrey's drawings of South XXXVI–VII might possibly be lyres. The section he has drawn stops short of the next preserved slab, but a fragment suggests that there were tray-bearers here, as on the north.

At the front of the procession on both south and north come beasts for sacrifice and the young men leading them. Animal sacrifice was a regular part of most Greek religious festivals. They were killed at the open-air altars, which were smeared with the blood, and then the inedible parts were burned on the altar for the deity while the rest feasted the participants. It will be noticed that there has been a rearrangement in this part of the south frieze since the numbers were originally allotted to slabs and figures. There is uncertainty over the ordering of these fragmentary slabs, most of which were already fallen from the building when Elgin took them. The present sequence is more convincing than that followed when the numbering was done, and is probably in the main right, but the positioning of some pieces remains in doubt. A similar rethinking accounts for the omission of numbers 70 and 71 on the north frieze.

All the victims on the south side are cattle. The youths who drive them, like all the figures in front of the chariots, wear the long *himation* (cloak) wrapped round them. On most slabs the cattle are well-behaved and the youths move or stand quietly, decorously. On XXXIX, however, the beast has made a sudden rush forward. One youth (109), his garment falling from him, hangs back on the halter (which must once have been shown in paint), while another (111, largely lost), at the animal's head, is in violent movement, causing a boy in front (XL 112) to turn sharply, while the creature he is leading lifts its head – Keats' 'heifer lowing at the skies'.

XXXVI 98 99 100 101 102 103 XXXVII 104 105 (gap) XLI 116 117 118

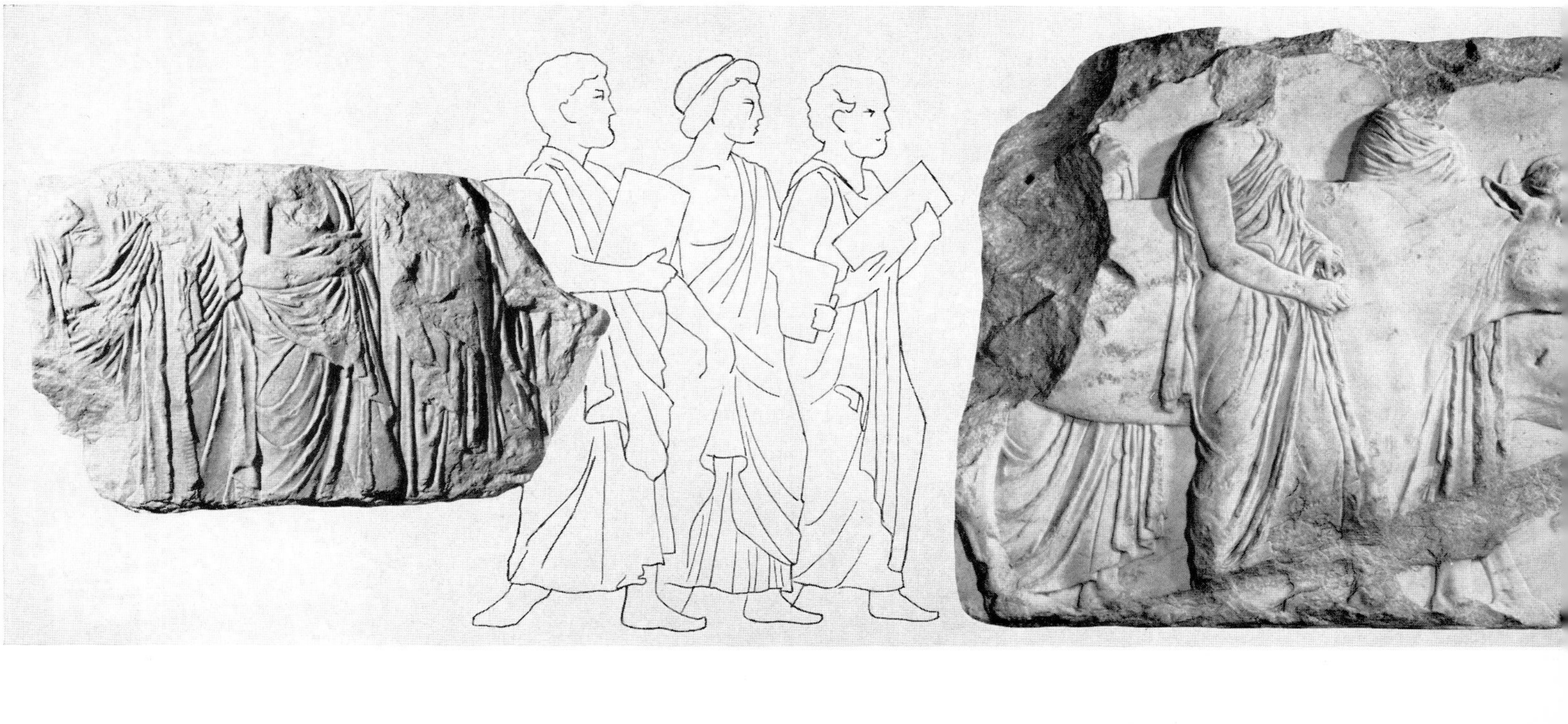

XXXIV 84 85 86 87 XXXV 88 89 90 91 92 93 94 95 96 97

9 (XLIII 125 - 6) XXXIX 109 110 111 XL 112 113 114 115

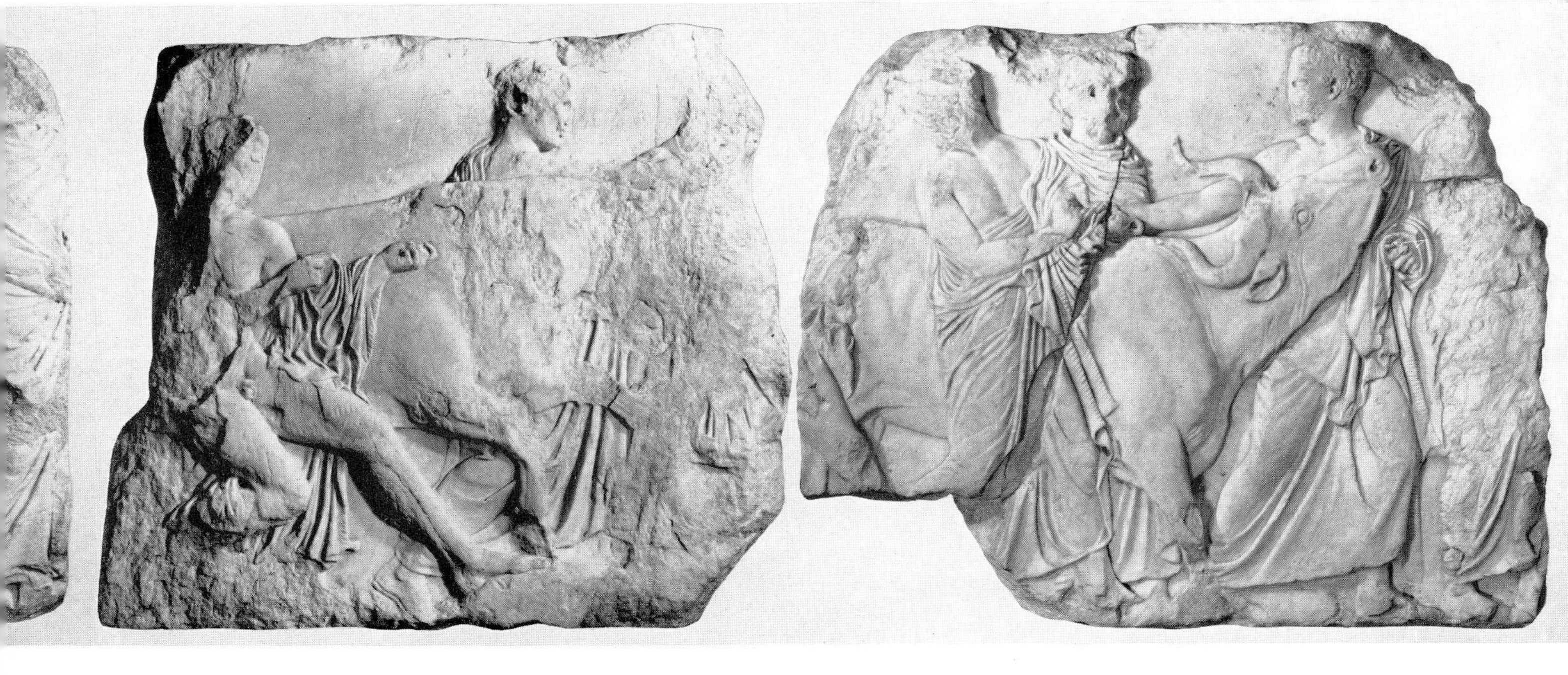

XLII 120 121 122 123 124 XXXVIII 106 107

SOUTH

EAST

I 1 II 2 3 4 5 6 III 7 8 9

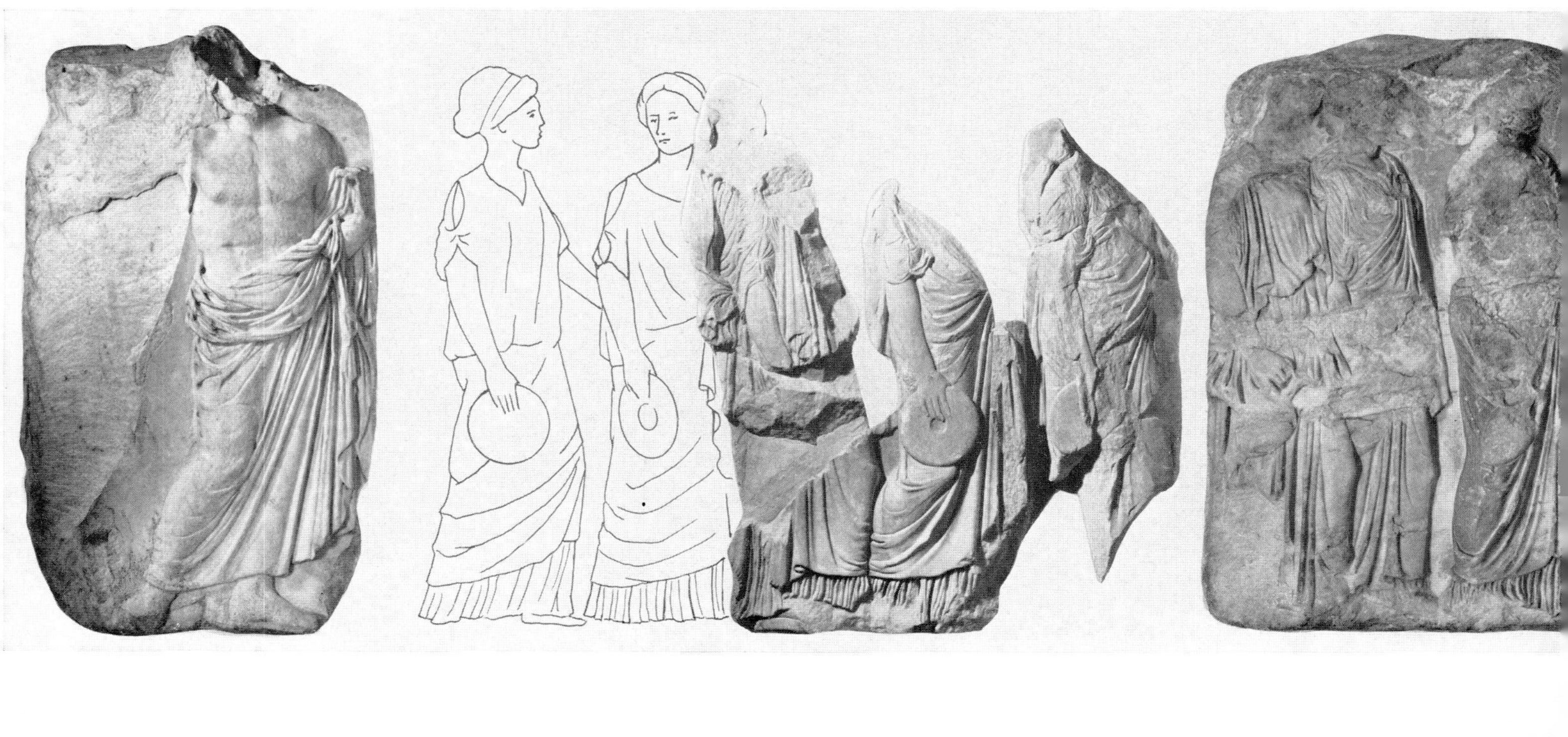

108 XLIII 127 128 XLIV 129 130 131

The first figure on the east frieze, carved on the return of the last block on the south, is a man in a *himation*, standing quietly and gesturing back, to form a link with the long side. He is a marshal, one of those in charge of ordering the procession. There are very many scattered throughout its length, though we have not had occasion to remark on them. After him the make-up of the procession changes in a significant way. On west, north and south the participation (*pace* Carrey's impression of South XXXVI–VII) is exclusively male. The head of the procession, shown at the two ends of the east front, is made up (apart from marshals) wholly of girls. Those to the south (II and III) are shown partly in single file, partly in pairs; and the same is true, though the actual disposition is different, of those to the north on slabs VII and VIII. It is possible that the marshals are to be thought of as ordering them all into pairs, but one cannot be sure of this. Those at the back, 2–6 and 60–3, carry in their right hands empty *phialai* (shallow libation-bowls; 55 also has one). Others further forward (7–10 and 58–9) have jugs. On vases it is common to see one figure (mortal or deity, for the gods too make libations) pouring wine from such a jug into a *phiale* held by another, or standing by with the jug while the other tips the libation from the bowl on to the ground or an altar-fire. One girl (57) carries an incense-burner, and in other cases it is not possible to make out what is carried, but only the front pair to the south (16–17) and the front two pairs to the north (50–1 and 53–4) seem to be empty-handed.

Between the foremost girls and the two groups of seated gods come thirteen figures (six to the south, seven to the north) of men, of varying ages, wearing *himatia*, standing quietly in casual groups. The interpretation of these is among the most controversial things in the study of the frieze, and there can be no certainty. The northernmost (VII 49) is addressing the first pair of girls and is surely inseparable from 52, who is addressing the second pair; both men must be marshals. A slab-division comes behind 49, and the corresponding division to the south separates two pairs carved with the gods on slab IV (20–3) from a pair (18–19) at the end of the slab with the girls. It is natural, I think, to see 18 and 19 as marshals, corresponding to, though differently arranged from, 49–52, in conversation with one another instead of with the girls, only the front two of whom form a pair (16–17), empty-handed like

10 11 12 13 14 15 16 17 18 19

IV 20 21 22 23 24 25
EAST

50–1 and 53–4. This leaves ten standing men carved on slabs IV and VI with the gods, and it is extremely tempting to see them as the Eponymous Heroes of the ten Attic tribes, forming a transition between the mortals in the procession and the gods. The ten tribes were an integral part of the constitution of Clisthenes (*c.* 505 B.C.), an essential element in the machinery of government; and the statues of the Eponymous Heroes formed one of the major monuments in the Athenian Agora. The figures on the frieze could well at the same time represent the citizens of Attica, in their tribes, waiting to watch the procession pass, and so make, at a different level, a transition between the procession shown forming by the Dipylon, and the little scene (isolated by the presence of the gods) taking place on the Acropolis in anticipation of the procession's arrival.

Twelve gods are shown seated, six on either side of the central scene, facing out towards the heads of the procession. With them are two winged children: Eros (42) leaning against his mother's knees at the outer end of the northern group, and on the south the messenger-girl Iris (28) standing beside Hera, with whom she is often associated. The other divine messenger, Hermes, unlike Iris (or Eros), is himself an Olympian, and is shown here seated, nearest the procession to the south (24). The concept of Twelve Olympians was known already at this time, and must certainly have been in the designer's mind, but he has departed in one particular from the canonical list. The Twelve are six gods and six goddesses, and here on the north we see three of each, but on the south are only two goddesses and a fourth god. The goddess omitted is Hestia (Vesta, goddess of the Hearth), most rarely imaged of Greek deities, who, so Plato says, used to stay at home when the others went abroad. Her place is taken by Dionysus, who was never an Olympian but often shown in their company.

The deities, though seated, occupy the full height of the slabs, and so are on a larger scale than the mortals. They sit on simple stools, and turn and gossip among themselves, like the heroes if so they be. Indications of their identity are discreet but sufficient. Hermes wears boots and his sun-hat lies on his knees. He once held something of

V 30 31 32 33 34 35

26 27 V 28 29 30 31

metal, no doubt his wand. He sits on a small cloak, which he has wrapped over his thighs, but is otherwise naked. The god who is back to back with him (the only one in either group to sit away from the procession) turns and leans his right arm on Hermes' shoulders. His left hand is raised and must have rested on a staff indicated in paint, no doubt a thyrsus, since this must be Dionysus. Like most of the gods he wears a *himation*, dropped from his shoulders and wrapped round his lower part. Next comes a goddess, a torch on her left arm, so Demeter, her chin resting on her hand. She seems in a further plane, overlapped both by Dionysus and by Ares, who sits next, both feet off the ground, the left ankle resting on his spear-shaft, which must have leant against his shoulder, mainly indicated in paint, his hands clasping his right knee. Both deities' attitudes – chin on hand and clasped knee – are associated in Greek art, from a generation before this, with brooding and melancholy. In Demeter's case one thinks of her mourning her lost daughter; and Ares, War, is a gloomy god, for whom this posture becomes habitual in later art. Next comes the standing Iris, overlapped by the knees of her mistress, who turns, lifting her veil in a bridal gesture commonly associated with her, to the Father of Gods and Men, whose massy figure backs on the central scene. The corresponding position to the north is occupied by the goddess of the temple, Athena, whose birth from Zeus' head was shown in the pediment above. Her aegis lies in her lap and she once held a bronze spear, but has no helmet or shield. She slightly overlaps a bearded god, who turns to her, her craftsman-colleague Hephaestus. He leans on a stick under his right armpit, a delicate allusion to his lameness. Separated from these by a little space come the last four, each slightly overlapping the next: Poseidon, young Apollo turning to talk to him, his twin sister Artemis, and (a very ruined, fragmentary group) Aphrodite with Eros at her knee. Her left hand lies on his shoulder, seeming to point out the procession to him, and he holds a parasol. In the Panathenaic procession daughters of metics were allowed to walk behind daughters of citizens, holding parasols over them; and this no doubt was in the designer's mind.

36 37 VI 38 39 40 (41)

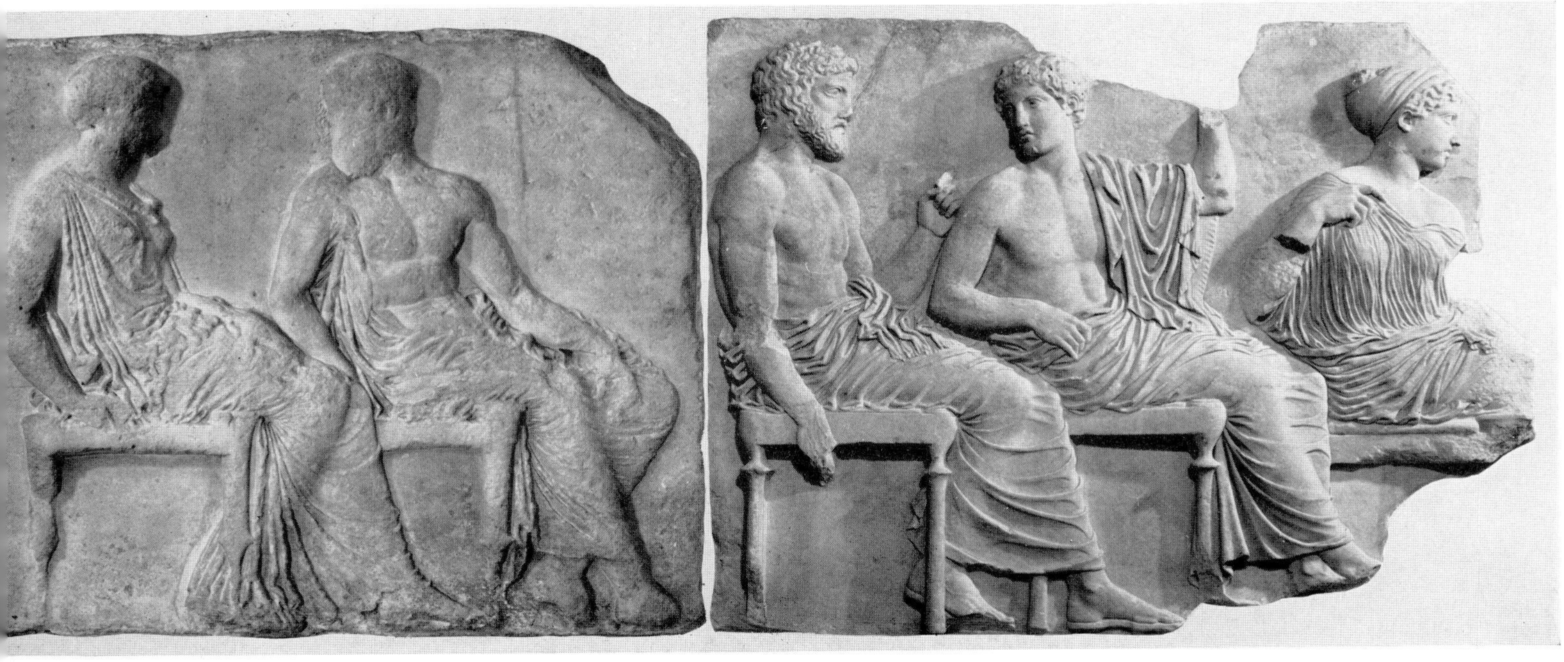

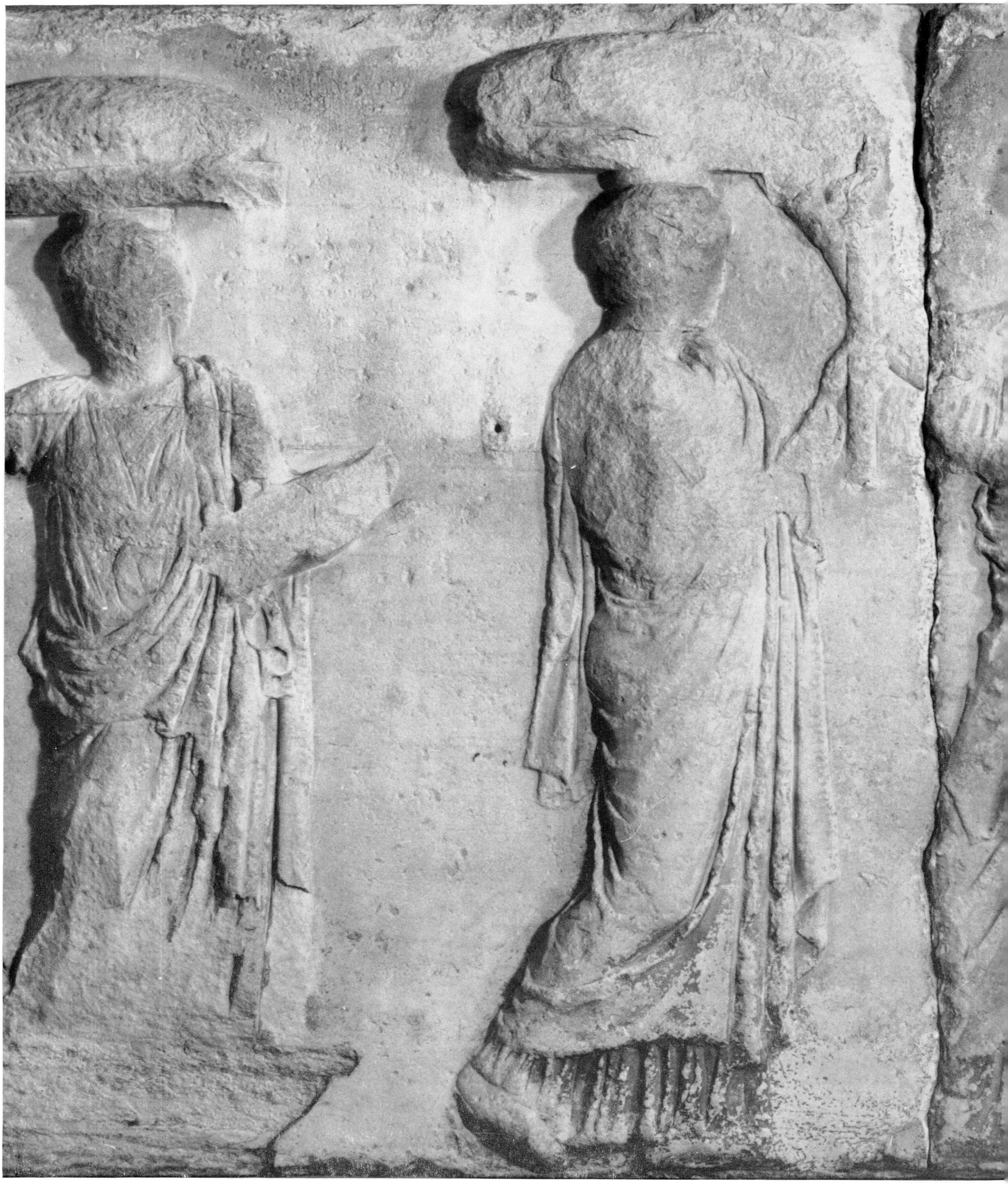

4 East V 31–5 The central mystery: priestess and girls with stools; the *archon basileus* and the child with the robe. The robe itself was always woven with a design of the Battle of Gods and Giants (shown also on the metopes at the east end of the temple) and it may be that the woven design was rendered here in paint. In spite of defacements these quiet groups of intent, detached figures are of great power. The artist here seems deliberately to reject the technical virtuosity he can sometimes display with such skill, preferring to invest this scene with a sober grace. Details **5–6, 9, 11,** and **14** show his brilliant side. Those at **12** and **13** are nearer to the mood shown here, but this seems the quietest, most restrained of all.

VI 42 43 44 45 46 47 48 VI

EAST

The central scene, the ritual handing over of the *peplos*, is discussed in the text, but there is one further question: the sex of the child helping with the robe (35). It is regularly called a boy, and there is an obvious likeness to the last figure on the north frieze (134), the little boy adjusting his master's or friend's belt. The pronounced Venus rings on the neck of the first child, however, suggest a girl, which perhaps, as girls wove and carried the robe, one might expect. The naked boy on the north has a cloak, his own or more likely the Knight's, thrown over his shoulder. The child on the east wears a garment fastened on both shoulders. The Doric *chiton* or *peplos* was so fastened and hung open at the side. On a lovely tombstone in New York from Paros a small girl, bending her head to kiss one of a pair of doves she carries, wears it so, and one sees the contour of her bare bottom in the opening. If she leant back like the child on the frieze she would reveal as much of her body, though the dress would still hang nearer the ground.

VIII 57 58 59 60 61 IX 62 63

49 50 51 52 53 54 55 56 VIII 57 58

From this point we follow the procession down again from the front, in the order it would have appeared to us had we waited to watch it pass. Round the corner from the girls on the east frieze come, as on the south, young men driving victims for sacrifice. The first block on the north is lost, but is recorded in drawings by Carrey and others. On its eastern return appeared not a marshal, as at the other end of the east frieze, but the last two girls in the procession; but the first figure on the north, standing quietly with his back to the corner, in front of the first heifer, looking back down the line, was surely a marshal rather than one of the herd-boys. Again, most of the animals go quietly, but one on slab II throws up head and fore-feet, and the boy on the far side of her (5) steps sharply forward, letting his garment drop from his shoulders. The cattle here are followed by a pair of horned sheep.

RTH

1 2 II 3 4 5

II 5 III 6 7 8 9 I

NORTH

The presence of the animals makes for considerable overlapping and massing of figures in this area, and the section ends with a marshal (12) backing closely on the last herd and looking the other way towards a file of more openly and evenly spaced figures carrying ritual objects. First are three tray-bearers, the foremost (13) carved on the same slab as the marshal and like him much ruined, the other two lost but recorded in a drawing. Next comes a well-preserved and most beautiful slab (VI) with four pitcher-bearers. Three have the jar already hoisted on the left shoulder, where they hold it with the right arm brought over the head, the front two steadying it below with the left hand – the vessels are clearly full. The fourth is stooping to lift his from the ground. His body is largely hidden by the drapery hanging from the forearms of a piper whose hands and pipes are carved on this slab. The rest of this more close-set group of four pipers, and the first two of four widely spaced lyre-players behind them, were on a slab which is lost and only known in Carrey's drawing, but the second pair of lyre-players is poorly preserved (VIII 26 and 27) with the first of a group of elders.

Lyre and double pipes are the two principal musical instruments of the Greeks. They appear together already in a sacrificial scene on a painted sarcophagus from late Bronze Age Crete, and the double pipe a millennium before that in a marble figurine from the Cyclades, but the accompanying stringed instrument there is the harp. The lyres on the frieze are of the largest, most elaborate type, the cithara, regularly used in musical contests and on ceremonial occasions.

VI 16 17 18 19 VII 20 21 22 23 24

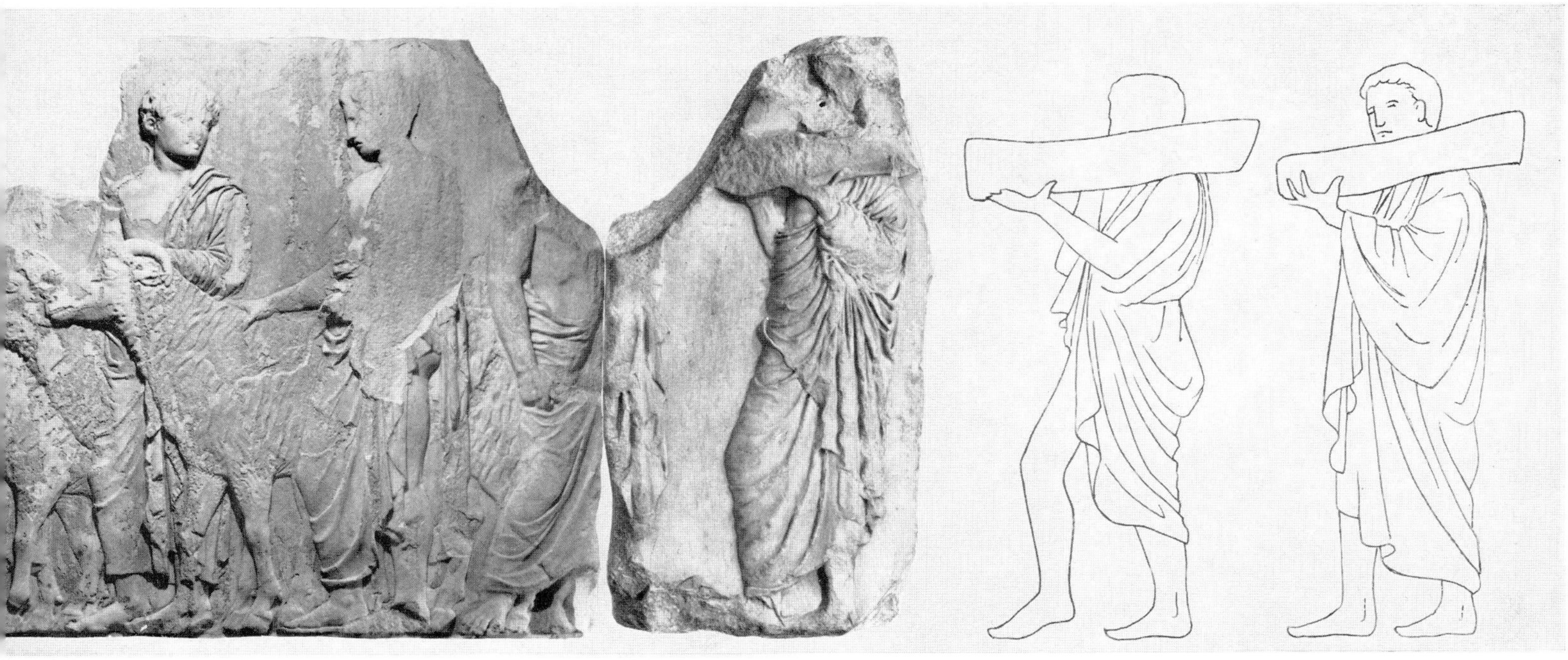

10 11 12 V 13 14 15

25 VIII 26 27 28 IX 29 30 31 32 33 34

IX 34 35 36 37 X 38 39 40 41 42 43 XI 44

NORTH

As on the south, much of the area with elders is lost, but one slab (x) is relatively well-preserved. The figures, in mantles wrapped round the lower body and over one shoulder, are conversationally grouped, some turning towards us. The physical structure of all figures in this art is strongly idealized, but the ideal is subtly modified, and here, in figures 38 and 39, there is a distinct if muted suggestion of the heavier forms of age.

Next come the chariots, those in front in movement, the last at rest, interspersed with many figures of marshals, some quiet, some gesturing, some in postures of violent action. The splendid group of slab xi–xii (44–7) is repeated with subtle variations on xvii–xviii (58–61) and these seem to have served as a model for one of the artists of the Great Altar of Pergamum, two and a half or three centuries later, where on the south frieze a long-robed charioteer, perhaps Helios, drives down a giant.

XIII 48 49 50 XIV

XII 45 46 47 XIII

51 52 53 XV 54 55

XV

NORTH

54 55 XVI

Another certainly deliberate echo of the chariot-scenes on the frieze is seen in two small Athenian reliefs, almost identical, which decorated bases of late fifth- or fourth-century date, one found on the Acropolis, the other built into the wall through the Agora, flung up in the third century A.D. to defend the shrunken city after the sack by the Herulians. Both must have supported dedications made by victors in the *apobasis*, the contest (illustrated in this part of the frieze) in which the Knight, wearing a helmet and carrying a shield, leaped in and out of the chariot. Writers speak of this as an event in the Panathenaic games, and without evidence of the frieze we should not have guessed that it formed part of the actual procession. Did it so? Or is this another instance of the generalizing tendency we meet so often in this art? Games and procession alike were aspects of the celebration of the holy feast, and the designer may have chosen to conflate them at this point in this way.

XIX 62 63 (XX)

XVII 56 57 58 XVIII 59 60 61

XXI

XXII 64 65 66

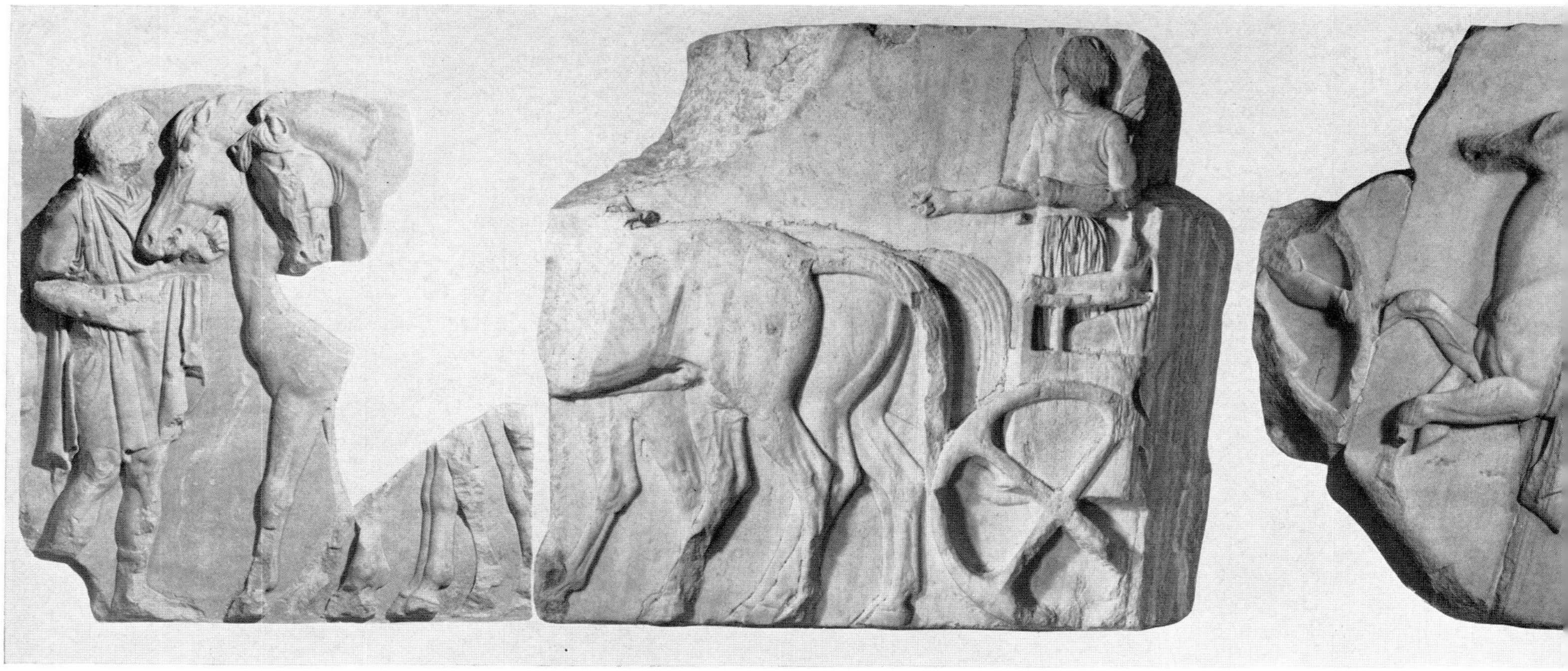

XXII 66 XXIII 67 68 XXIV 69

NORTH

The musicians, the elders and the front part of the cavalcade have suffered on this side from the explosion much as the corresponding stretch of the south side has, but rather more here remains aesthetically coherent. The rear three-quarters of the northern cavalcade is among the best preserved and justly most renowned parts of the frieze. The artist chose here to give a spectacular demonstration of his skill in grouping and varying overlapping masses within the shallow depth of his relief. The composition is controlled by a brilliant use of near-repetition of subtly varied figures. A particularly telling example is the boy turning on his horse and looking back, his left arm back and down: XXIX 88, XXXIII 103, XXXVI 111. All these are naked, but there are two variants: XXXI 96, in a tunic, who does not turn so far; XLI 129, muffled in his cloak, who turns right back but keeps his left hand forward on the rein.

(XXVII 81–4) XXVIII 85 86 87 XXIX 88 89 90

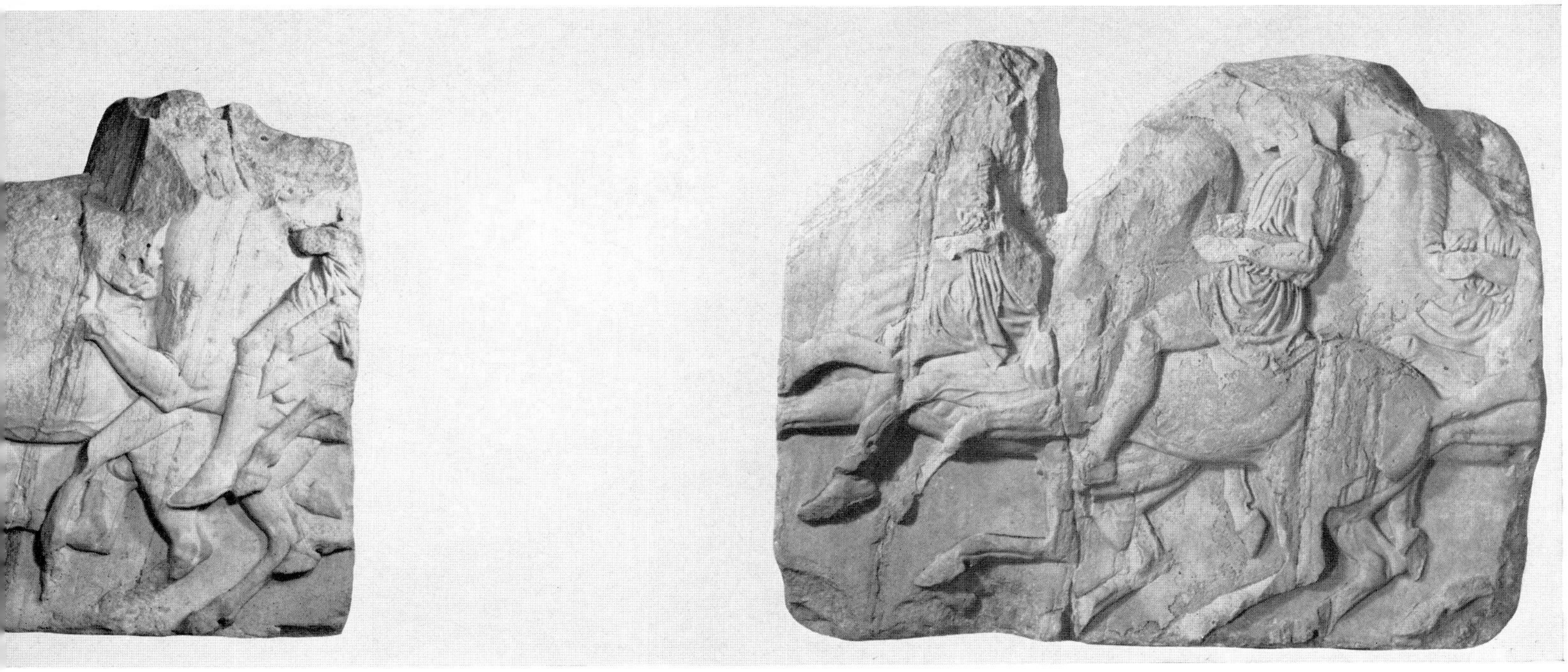

72 73 74 (XXV 75-7) XXVI 78 79 80

91 XXX 92 93 XXXI 94 95 96 97

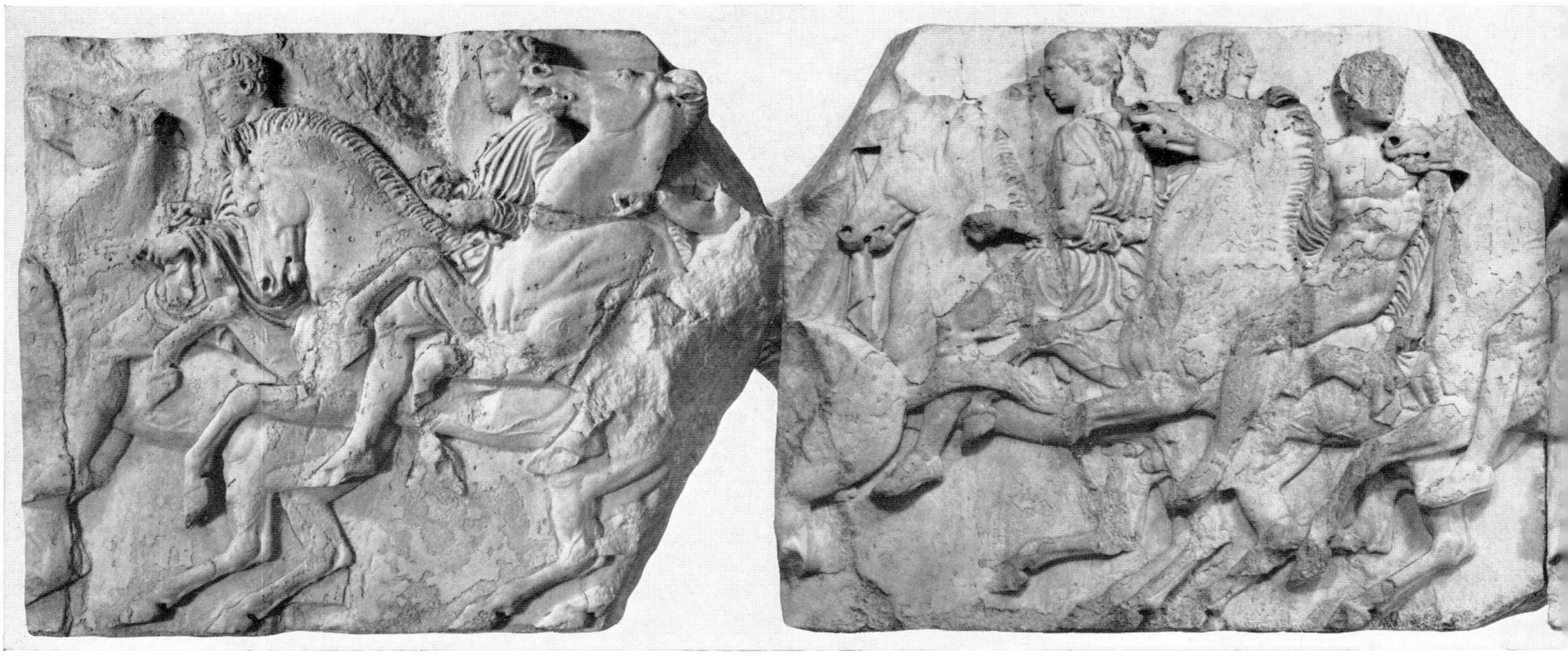

XXXII 98 99 100 XXXIII 101 102 103

NORTH

None of these riders is armoured and most are bare-headed, but towards the rear are some in skin caps (xxxviii-ix, 116, 117 and 120). There is another further forward (xxxv 108) and there may have been more in the more damaged areas in front, but none here is preserved with the broad-brimmed sun-hat worn by several on south and west. Most keep a level look, but variety and charm is achieved by the occasional bent head. The classical convention admits little modification of the ideal type. Feature for feature these youths hardly differ among themselves, nor do the marshals or other bearded figures, nor the girls of the east front. Expressiveness is evoked by the whole attitude of the figure and especially by the angle of the head, as it surely was in the masked actors who played in the theatre of Dionysus below the Acropolis to the south. Aeschylus had died in 456, but his dramas continued in production after his death. Sophocles, a personal friend of Pericles, with whom he was elected general in 440 while the Parthenon was being built, had won his first dramatic victory in 468. Euripides first competed in 455 and won his first victory in 441. Attic tragedy and the Parthenon are facets of one world.

XXXVI 111 112 XXXVII 113 114 115

XIV 104 105 106 XXXV 107 108 109 110 XXXVI

XXVIII 116 117 118 119 XXXIX 120 121 122 XL

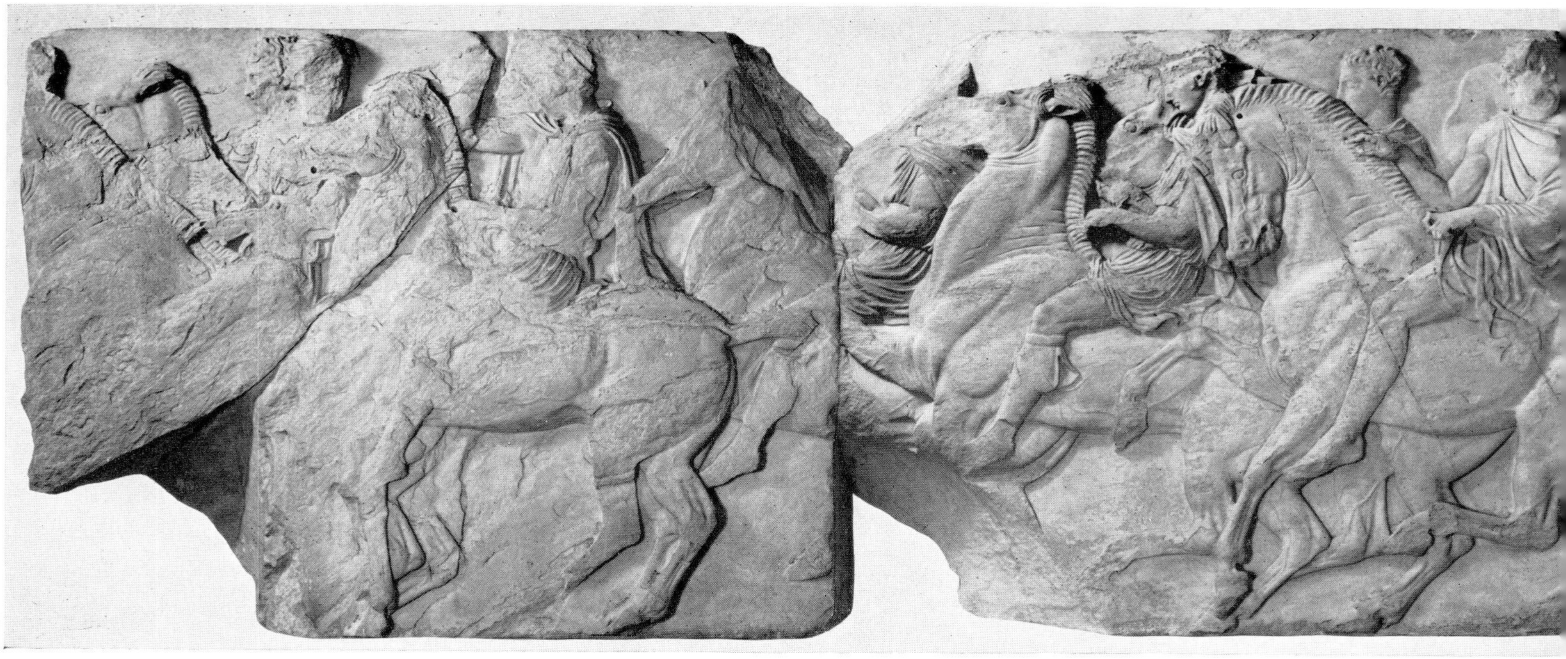

XL 123 124 125 XLI 126 127 128 129

NORTH

A figure on the last slab (XLII 131) is reminiscent at the same time of the naked rider turning and of another striking rider (XXXVIII 118) who turns his naked back to us as he raises his right arm; but 131 is not a rider. He stands by his mount, as does 133 on the same slab, the tunicked youth whose belt is being tied by the last figure, the little boy; and 133's bent head again picks up a recurrent accent among the riders: 127, 120, 116, 98, 97, 79. In the further plane, 132 and (almost totally concealed) 130, are already up, part of the cavalcade, but these figures in the foreground getting themselves ready make a transition to the west frieze.

WEST

I 1 II 2 3 III 4

XLII 130 131 132 133 134

The first figure on the west, carved on the return of the last slab of the north frieze, is a marshal, still, facing out from the procession, very like the one at the opposite corner of the building, on the eastern return of the last south slab. The next slab (II) interchanges, as it were, with the last of the north, showing two riders already up. The one in front, naked but for his cloak, turns back, his left arm bent sharply up, echoing the movement of the dismounted North 131 even more closely than the riders on the north which we noticed he resembled. These two scarcely overlap; and in general on the west there is none of the massing that marks the treatment of the cavalry on the long sides. The composition is more open and more broken, but controlled in the same way by repetition of variations on certain striking types. This slab is in the British Museum, the rest still on the building. Slab III has a horse standing between its master at its head and a naked groom behind, while a marshal hurries past looking back. The master (4), naked but for a cloak, has his hands up by the horse's muzzle but looks away. He stands frontal, his right arm brought across his body, and this pose is repeated with variations in 9 (the arm not brought across), 22, and (closest to 4) the last figure of all (30), carved on the return of the first southern slab.

Two riders are shown on slab IV, the second (8), who wears a cap with a flying tail, being bearded. Slab V has two Knights, one (9) standing naked by his mount, the second, in a tunic, already up, followed on VI by another, who is cuirassed and helmeted. The figure behind him (12) also wears a helmet but is naked except for his cloak. He is not mounted and his horse is not shown. He stoops to adjust his sandal, his foot up on a prominent rock, and he is turned in the opposite direction to the general movement, one of several such sharp accents in the composition of this frieze. Rocks are shown at points on the long sides, but with nothing like the scale and emphasis given to this and to a second on the west which serves the same purpose (29).

5 6 IV 7 8 V

V 9 10 VI 11 12

WEST

After two more riders on slab VII, slab VIII shows a single horse and man, isolated, the horse rearing, the man on foot, leaning back and trying to rein it down. He is a powerful, dramatic figure, his left arm out and back, cloak and cap-tail flying. His face is lost, but Elgin's cast shows that he was bearded. This magnificent group comes almost in the centre, and of the Knights only this one and 8, who wears the same long-tailed cap, have beards. We know that each year there were two hipparchs to command the Knights, and perhaps these are they.

VIII 15 IX 16 17

VII 13 14 VIII 15

X 18 19 XI 20 21

XI 20 21 XII 22 23 2

WEST

Follow three slabs (IX–XI) each with two riders: 16 and 17 in wide-brimmed hats, 18, 19, and 21 bare-headed, 20 helmeted. The next (XII) has one of the most attractive groups. The horse has put its head right down, muzzle between forelegs, and the beautiful curve of the maned neck is framed between two Knights standing quietly: 22 naked, an arm brought across his body, looking down; 23 in a tunic, face and arm raised. A little boy stands at the horse's tail.

The horses on XIII and XIV are restive, difficult. With his wide hat slung at his back 25 stands by his steed reining its head down, while behind him another horse rears unchecked, its master (26) having turned to help another with his, which is rearing in the opposite direction – another of the divisive accents which characterize this western frieze. The Knight (27) is a splendid figure, very like some of the marshals among the chariots on the north. Later in the century 25 and his horse were copied by a painter of a small red-figure vase; the most direct but by no means the only reminiscence of the frieze in that medium.

On slab XV all is quiet: two horses standing, a ruined figure (28), perhaps groom rather than Knight, at the head of the first. Beside the second its master (29) faces the opposite way, his foot up on a rock to adjust his sandal, like 12 but bare-headed. The whole is closed by the beautiful figure mentioned in connection with 4, a naked youth standing frontal, his cloak on his left arm stretched high up, the right brought across the body. He looks as though he had just got up, stretching in the dawn of this festal day.

XIV 26 27 XV 28 29

XIII 25 XIV 26 27

XVI 30

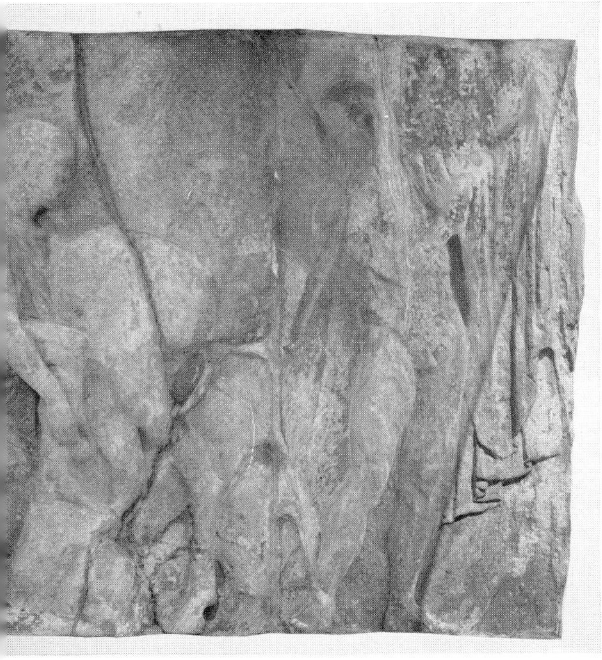

5 North XLII 130–2 This shows part of the westernmost slab on the north side. The figures in the background are already up, but the central youth still stands beside his mount, like so many of those in the west frieze. The other horse too, only the forehand of which appears in this picture, is waiting while its master has his belt tied by a little boy. The knight's gesture, turning with his left hand raised to his head, is repeated by several of those already on horseback. It is perhaps a signal.

6 West II 2 This figure, from the northernmost slab of the west frieze, is an example of the signalling rider. The slab, with its riders already up, balances the scene of preparation in the last, completing the *enjambement* of north and west, the west mainly preparation, the north mainly riders in movement. The two youths in these two details, with their three-quartered faces and the complex movement of their naked bodies, illustrate the consummate mastery of the technique of low relief, with its subtlety and range, combining the skills of carving and drawing. The young man here wears his hair rather longer than many of his companions. There is some variety, but all have it more or less short. Since the Persian Wars really long hair for men had not been in fashion.

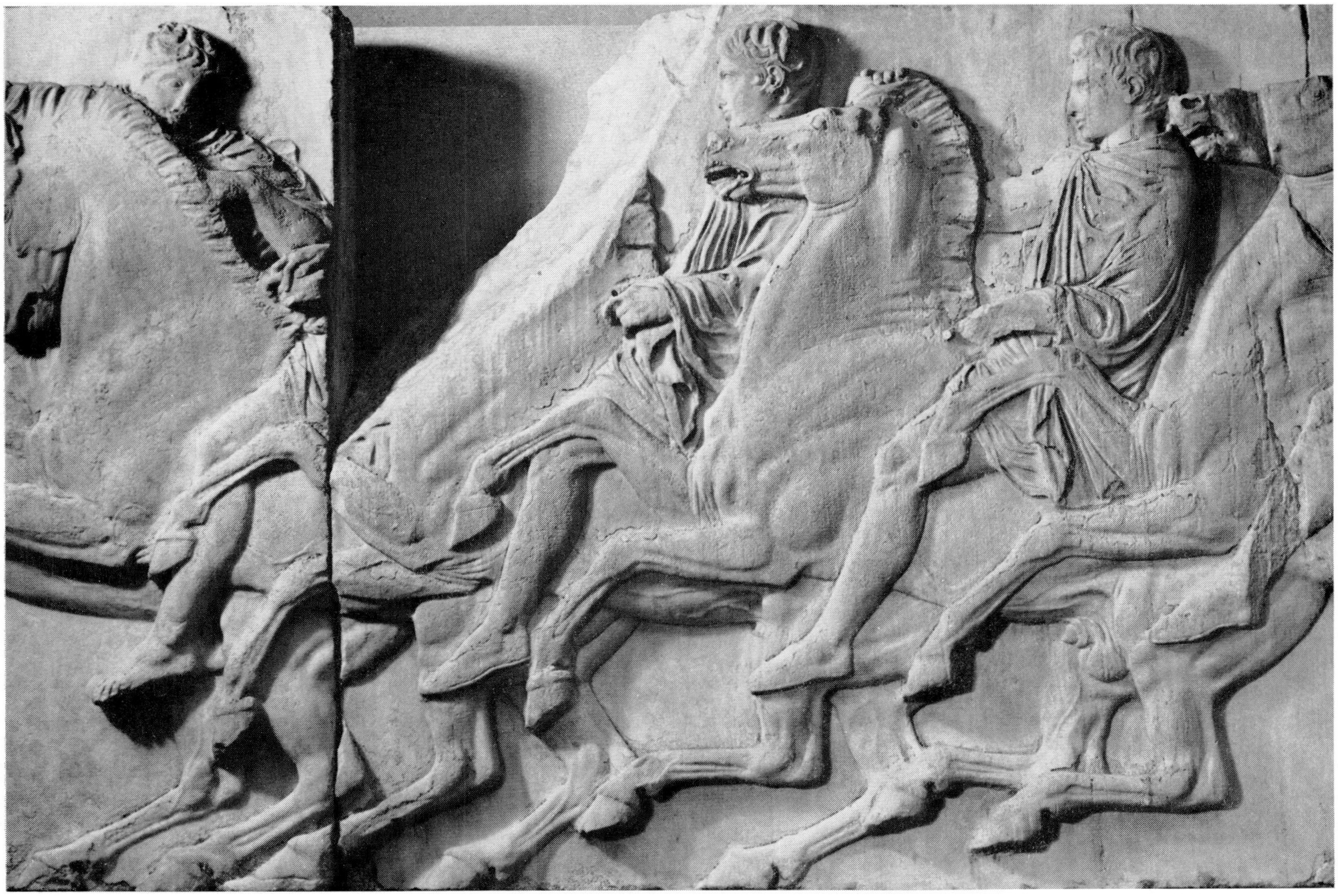

7 and **8** North XXXVI–VII 112–15 (detail of 114 *left*) This is one of the best preserved and most attractive stretches of the cavalcade. The horsemen are less closely massed than in some areas, and they overlap each other fairly regularly, so that the pattern of men's and horses' legs across the lower part of the slabs, though it is subtly varied, has an easily apprehended rhythm. In contrast with the beautiful naked torsos in the last details, set off against floating cloaks, these boys' bodies are muffled, or concealed by a companion's horse. They hold the reins (once added in bronze or paint) low in the left hand, and 115 reaches out his right and lays the fingers lightly on his horse's hogged mane, between the ears, soothing it. Part of the missing corner of slab XXXVII, with 113's head and most of the head of 114's mount, survives, somewhat battered, in Athens. The severe, lovely profile of 114 (shown in the detail) is a perfect example of the deliberately 'inexpressive' classical ideal, which yet achieves a kind of expressiveness in context, in spite of (or by reason of?) its calculated subordination in the design as a whole. One finds the same kind of effect in the work of some artists of other periods: Piero della Francesca, for instance, or Seurat. In classical Greece it is the rule.

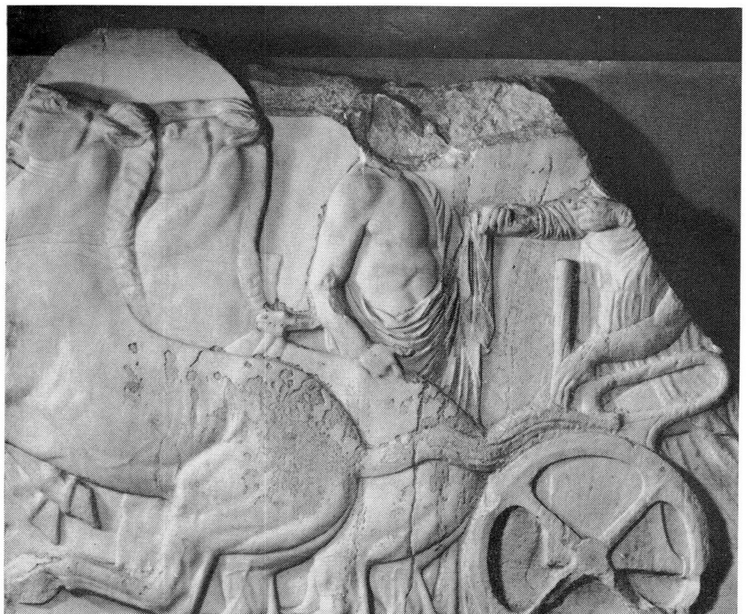

9 West XII 22–3 This beautiful slab is unusual in more than one respect. First, the horse is unique not only in its action but in the rendering of its conspicuous mane. Most of the Parthenon horses have the hogged mane which, vase-painting suggests, began to be fashionable in the later sixth century and is the regular thing in the fifth. Here the strands wave down over the neck. Then, which figure is the horse's master? I suppose the one in the tunic standing by it; but the naked youth in front is not an attendant, like the boy at the horse's tail (not shown in this detail). He has no mount (the two horses on the next slab have riders up). Perhaps he is a marshal – some are young, but the rider's cloak instead of the heavy wrap is odd. By his look and the position of his hand he might be writing something down on a tablet, as in the *dokimasia* (inspection of young knights and their horses). Could he be booking the knight, whose gesture might be one of protest, for having his horse's mane wrongly dressed? The horse registers indifference.

10 North XVIII 59–61 One might think this car had only two horses, but a third is glimpsed above the rear one's head, a fourth on the next slab. The charioteer's hands are forward with the reins. The arm below is the warrior's, catching the rail as he jumps in. This seems one of the more workaday bits of carving on the frieze, not the equal of either of those illustrated above and opposite, yet the comparison underlines the high and steady level.

11 West VIII 15 Rearing horse and straining master (foot braced on a rock) are carved with more particularity – taut muscles, veins – than most on the frieze. Despite the different technique (relief against statue) and scale, Carrey's drawing and the fragments suggest that this splendid image has some of the character of the great chariot-teams of the gods in the west gable.

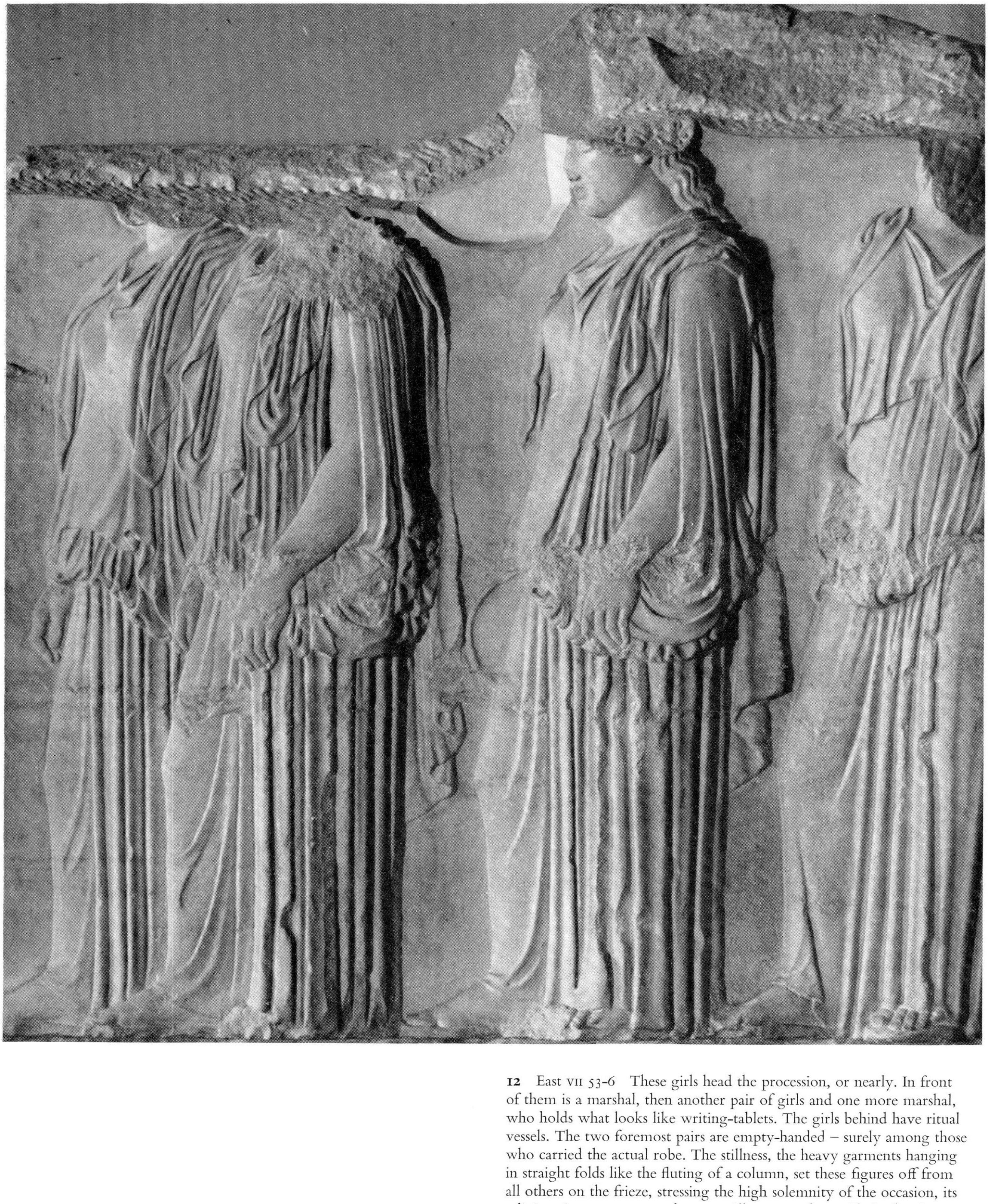

12 East VII 53-6 These girls head the procession, or nearly. In front of them is a marshal, then another pair of girls and one more marshal, who holds what looks like writing-tablets. The girls behind have ritual vessels. The two foremost pairs are empty-handed – surely among those who carried the actual robe. The stillness, the heavy garments hanging in straight folds like the fluting of a column, set these figures off from all others on the frieze, stressing the high solemnity of the occasion, its religious importance, as other parts illustrate rather pride in the city or the spirit of the holiday. This beautiful slab, which had fallen from the building, was dug up in 1789 and bought by the great collector Choiseul-Gouffier, then French ambassador in Constantinople. It is now in the Louvre.

13 North VI 17-20 The youths with horses or chariots wear a small cloak fastened at the throat and floating, and under it nothing or the short *chiton*. Those making music, carrying ritual vessels or driving beasts for sacrifice, functions more directly related to the religious occasion, have the ampler *himation*. We have many vessels of just the form these boys are carrying, in clay and, as these are no doubt deemed, in metal, and many pictures of girls filling them at the fountain (woman's work; when boys carry them it seems always, as here, a special case), and we know certainly for once the name the Greeks used for the shape: *hydria*. Girls carry them on the head, often without hands; these youths, less practised, on the shoulder. The last stoops to lift his, and overlapping him comes the first piper. A charming group.

14 and **15** East VI 38-40 Three of the group of six seated deities to the spectator's right. Behind them, backing on the central scene, are Athena and Hephaestus, in front Aphrodite, accompanied by her son Eros. The two young people are certainly the twin brother and sister, Apollo and Artemis. There is nothing now to identify the kingly bearded figure, but by a process of elimination he must be Zeus' brother Poseidon, lord of the sea. The staff he held in his left hand will have ended in a trident-head. Both he and Apollo wear the *himation*, Apollo's brought up over the left shoulder, Poseidon's wrapped only about his lower body. Artemis wears the *himation* similarly wrapped over her crinkly *chiton*, which she is pulling up as it slips from her shoulders. *Himation* over ankle-length *chiton* is common wear for women, as for older men, and that is probably what is meant here, though Artemis the huntress can wear a short *chiton* like the Knights of the frieze; and even here her hair is scarfed up, as though ready for the windy chase. This beautiful and beautifully preserved profile is another example of the 'expressive inexpressiveness' of the classical ideal. Compare the head in detail **7**. Feature for feature the lineaments of the mortal boy are almost those of the girl-goddess; both are without definable expression; yet they tell quite differently (and both most effectively) in their different contexts. The brother and sister, Apollo and Artemis, are the closest pairing among the gods, constantly associated with one another, and with their mother Leto (not an Olympian, so not here) whose wrongs they delight to avenge together; but here Apollo turns away to talk with Poseidon. There is a cunning variety in the decorative play of folds as the simple garment responds to the movements of the limbs beneath.

16 East VI 38 Here again, think away the beard and we have the same features, the same lack of defined expression, the same total rightness in its place. One little wrinkle on the brow is, apart from the beard, the only difference.

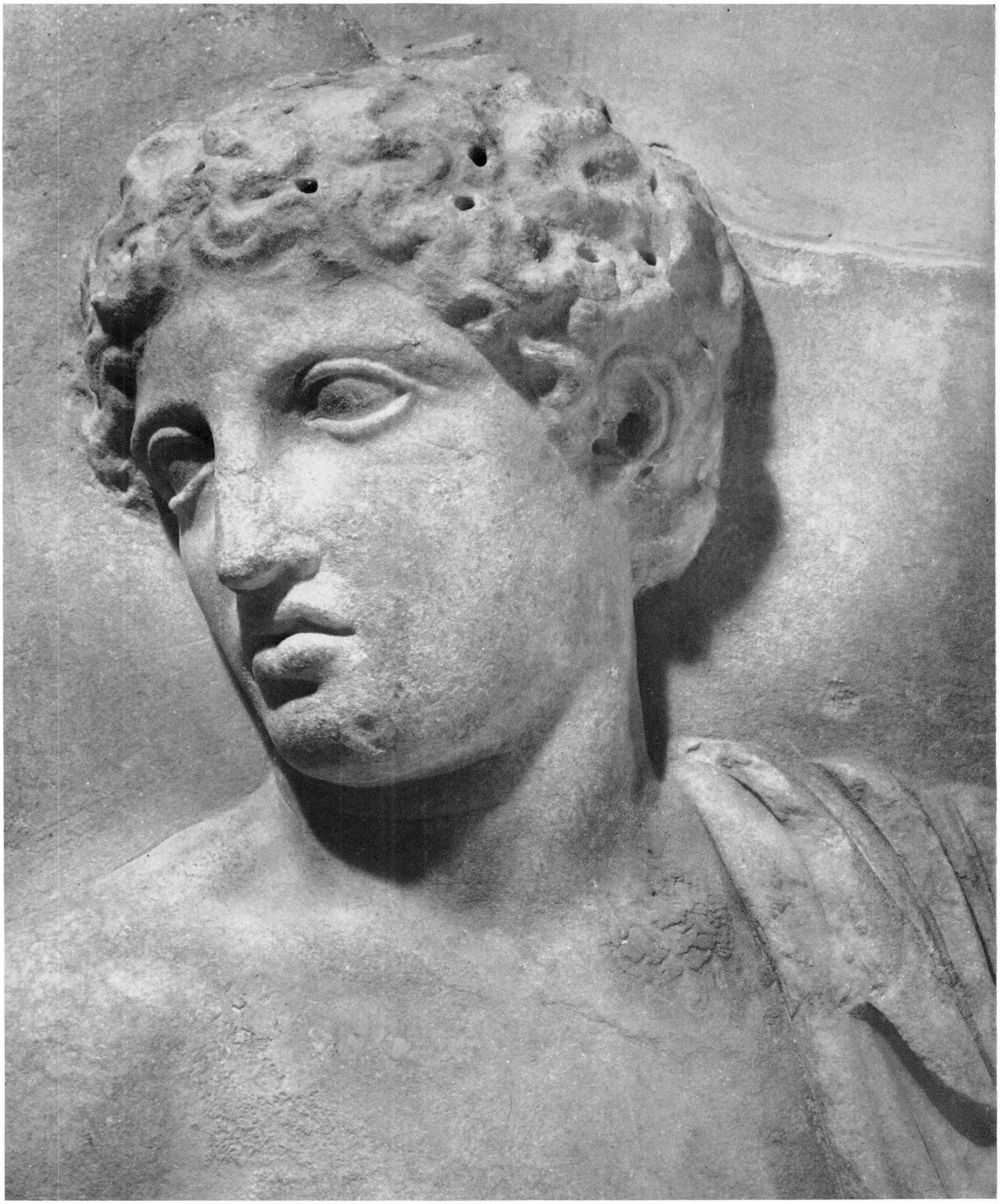

17 East VI 39 Here the schema is different, the head turned back, face in three-quarter view, but the ideal, 'inexpressive' features are the same. The hair is less realized than in the others, the ear too not fully carved, and drill-holes show that a wreath of metal was to hide much. Poseidon's hair too was prepared for a metal band, but a thin fillet cut into the locks.

18 North II (between 4 and 5) Animals other than horses have a small role in Greek monumental art, though the lovely seal- and coin-devices tell a different story. Still, Myron's most famed work was a bronze cow, set on the Acropolis at perhaps about the time of the Parthenon or a little before; and the cattle of the frieze, consummately modelled in lowest relief, are splendid.